TWAYNE'S WORLD AUTHORS SERIES

A Survey of the World's Literature

Sylvia E. Bowman, Indiana University

GENERAL EDITOR

RUSSIA

Nicholas P. Vaslef

EDITOR

Nikolay Karamzin

TWAS 250

Nikolay Karamzin

Nikolay Karamzin

By NATALYA KOCHETKOVA

Academy of Sciences of the USSR

Prepared for publication in cooperation with
Novosti Press Agency (APN)
Publishing House, USSR

TWAYNE PUBLISHERS

A DIVISION OF G. K. HALL & CO., BOSTON

Library of Congress Cataloging in Publication Data

Kochetkova, Nataliia.
  Nikolay Karamzin.

  (Twayne's world authors series; TWAS 250 : Russia)
  Bibliography: p.
  Includes index.
  1. Karamzin, Nikolaĭ Mikhaĭlovich, 1766-1826 —
Criticism and interpretation.
PG3314.Z8K6   891.7'8'209   70-188827
ISBN 0-8057-2488-5

Contents

About the Author

Natalya Kochetkova completed her studies in philology at Leningrad University in 1961. Following a period of postgraduate studies at the Institute of Russian Literature (Pushkin House), the Academy of Sciences of the U.S.S.R., she successfully defended her thesis for a master's degree in 1965, taking as her theme "N. M. Karamzin and Russian Poetry at the Close of the Eighties and First Half of the Nineties of the Eighteenth Century."

As a specialist in literature at Pushkin House, Natalya Kochetkova was involved in group research projects, notably for *The History of Russian Poetry* and *Literature and Folklore*. Her articles on Russian literature of the eighteenth century have been published in the literary series *Eighteenth Century* and in various journals and periodicals.

Preface

Nikolay Mikhaylovich Karamzin (1766–1826) belongs to the generation of Russian authors considered the precursors of Pushkin. The term refers both to the chronological sequence, for Karamzin was born thirty-five years before Pushkin, and to Karamzin's creative endeavors which, like those of a number of his contemporaries, in many respects paved the way for the development of Pushkin's rare talent.

"Words belong to a century—but ideas, to centuries," wrote Karamzin, and this aphorism applies partly to his own works. Karamzin's "words" need not be transposed into today's language, whereas the works of Russian authors appearing a few decades before his—or even concurrently—are impossible to read without special commentary. Karamzin is rightly considered a reformer of the Russian literary language, though in some respects he displayed excessive purism, resisting the introduction of colloquial speech into literature which so enriched the language of Krylov, Griboedov, and Pushkin.

In the evolution of the Russian literary language, the period connected with Karamzin's name coincided with Russian Sentimentalism. This literary trend, reaching its peak in Russia between 1790 and 1800, was most fully and richly expressed in Karamzin's works. It is natural, therefore, that Karamzin is recognized as having been the leading representative of Russian Sentimentalism. He was imitated and quoted, and epigraphs were often taken from his works. But at the same time, there were those who raised their voices in disapproval and who even considered Karamzin's works a bad influence on literature. Critics attacked Sentimentalism on various grounds and, naturally, criticism intensified when Realism began gaining a foothold in Russian literature.

By the time Pushkin had achieved maturity as a writer, many critics found Karamzin dull and uninteresting to read. The young Vissarion G. Belinsky in 1834, in a retort to the Sentimentalist's followers, argued with conviction that Karamzin's works "were already dead and would never rise again." But this opinion was provoked by Belinsky's desire to attract the attention of the reading public to contemporary works, especially Pushkin's, which were far from being understood or accepted by everyone. In time, Belinsky changed his attitude toward Karamzin, realizing that the writer had "led Russian literature into a sphere of new ideas."

Arguments about Karamzin continued, however, for years. For each new admirer there was a stern critic who accused Karamzin of being overly sentimental and affected. Nevertheless, his works kept coming out in new editions and were translated into English, German, French, Italian, and other languages.

As Belinsky put it, Karamzin "topped his contemporaries by a whole head," though one could scarcely say that he was ahead of his time. On the contrary, his merit lay in the fact that he was quick to realize the needs and issues of the times.

To properly understand him, Karamzin's writing career should be traced in chronological sequence, since—despite the diversity of his literary pursuits as a publicist and author of poems, tales, critical reviews, and a multi-volume history—a definite thread of unity runs throughout his works.

The material of this book is arranged in chapters which correspond to the important stages in Karamzin's career. Thus, the first chapter reviews the initial period of his writings—the time his literary interests were being formed. The second chapter focuses on the *Moscow Journal* (1791–92), the first independent periodical published by Karamzin, whose pages carried some of the works that brought him fame and recognition. One of them, *Letters of a Russian Traveller*, was so substantial in size and content that it deserves special commentary, because only part of the *Letters* appeared in the *Moscow Journal,* the rest being published in the course of the next few years. The third chapter, therefore, gives an analysis of the *Letters of a Russian Traveller.* Chapter Four is concerned with the period of Karamzin's literary career when he was undergoing a certain crisis of ideas, which did not, however, put a stop to his publishing or literary endeavors—the almanac *Aglaya*, the anthology of poetry entitled *Aonides*, and other publications from 1793 to 1799. Chapter Five is devoted to the journal, *The Messenger of Europe*, which Karamzin published in 1802 and 1803. The sixth chapter covers the longest period, since Karamzin worked on his *History of the Russian State* from 1804 to 1826. We review this multi-volume history only from the aspect most pertinent to this study, that is, as a work inseparable from belles-lettres.

NATALYA KOCHETKOVA

Chronology

1766   December 1 (12th, Julian calendar) Nikolay Mikhaylovich Karamzin born in village of Mikhaylovka, in former province of Simbirsk
(now Ulianovsk Region). Father was retired officer, Mikhail
Egorovich Karamzin; mother—Ekaterina Petrovna (née Pazu-
khina).

1770   After death of E. P. Karamzina, second marriage of his father.

1774   Registers for military service in army.

1781   Given rank of junior lieutenant.

1780–   Studies at Professor I. M. Schaden's pension in Moscow; attends
1783   lectures at Moscow University.

1783   In St. Petersburg becomes close friend of the poet I. I. Dmitriev.
Starts translating from German; first translation appears in print:
S. Gessner's idyll *Wooden Leg (Das Hölzerne Bein)*. Death of father.
In winter resigns from army as lieutenant; returns to Simbirsk.

1784   Moves to Moscow, becomes acquainted with N. I. Novikov and
other members of Friendly Learned Society; joins Moscow Masonic
Order; friendship with A. A. Petrov.

1786   Publishes his translation of A. von Haller's poem *On the Origin of
Evil (Vom Ursprung des Übels)*.

1786–   Contributes to journal, *Readings for Children for Their Hearts and
1789   Minds*. Later, assumes editorial responsibility for it, with A. A.
Petrov as co-editor.

1787   Publishes his translation of Shakespeare's *Julius Caesar*.

1788   Publishes his translation of Lessing's *Emilia Galotti*.

1789–   Tours Europe (Germany, Switzerland, France, and England);
1790   begins work on *Letters of a Russian Traveller*. Relations with the
Masons become cool on his return to Moscow. Prepares material
for *Moscow Journal*.

1791–   Publishes *Moscow Journal* which carries his tales *Poor Liza* and
1792   *Natalya, the Boyar's Daughter;* also first part of *Letters of a Russian
Traveller*. Government repressions against Masons begin.

1793   Death of his close friend A. A. Petrov.

1793–   Publishes almanac *Aglaya*, featuring verse and prose, including
1794   his tale *Bornholm Island* and continuation of *Letters of a Russian
Traveller*.

1794   Publishes first collected works, entitled *My Trifles*.

1795   Contributes to newspaper, *Moscow Gazette*.

1796   Death of Catherine II; Paul I ascends throne. Publishes short tale "Julia" and separate edition of *Poor Liza*.

1796– Publishes almanac of poetry, *Aonides*.
1799

1797– *Letters of a Russian Traveller* published in separate edition; also
1801   "Discourse on Happiness" and second edition of *My Trifles*.

1798   Publishes *Pantheon of Foreign Literature*.

1799– *Readings for Children for Their Hearts and Minds* published in
1803   second edition.

1800   Begins work on *Pantheon of Russian Authors*.

1801   Writes two odes to Alexander I; "A Word of Praise to the Empress Catherine II" published. In April, marries Elizaveta Ivanovna Protasova.

1801– Publishes second edition of *Moscow Journal*.
1802

1802   Publishes *Pantheon of Russian Authors*.

1802– Publishes *Messenger of Europe* which prints his *Martha the Mayor-*
1803   *ess; My Confession; A Knight of Our Times; The Emotional and the Cold, Two Characters*. Death of his wife in April 1802.

1803   October 31, appointed official historiographer by order of tsar. Begins work on *History of the Russian State*.

1803– Publishes first edition of collected works in eight volumes. Marries
1804   Ekaterina Andreevna Vyazemskaya.

1810   Travels to Tver to see Grand Duchess Ekaterina Pavlovna. Awarded Order of St. Vladimir, Third Class; promoted to rank of Collegiate Councillor.

1811   Writes *A Memoir on Ancient and Modern Russia* and reads it to Tsar Alexander I.

1812   Leaves Moscow just ahead of Napoleon's army; travels to Yaroslavl, and Nizhni Novgorod.

1813   Returns to Moscow, continues work on *History*.

1814   Publishes second revised edition of *Collected Works* in nine volumes.

1816   Moves to St. Petersburg. First volumes of *History of the Russian State* go to press. Awarded Order of St. Anne, promoted to rank of State Councillor. Publishes collection of *Various Tales*.

1818   First eight volumes of *History of the Russian State* published.

1818– New editions of earlier works published.
1824

1826   Dies on May 22 (June 3, Julian calendar). Buried in cemetery of Alexander Nevsky Monastery, St. Petersburg.

Transliteration Table*

	I	II			I	II
Аа	a	a		Рр	r	r
Бб	b	b		Сс	s	s
Вв	v	v		Тт	t	t
Гг	g	g		Уу	u	u
Дд	d	d		Фф	f	f
Ее	e[1]	e		Хх	kh	kh
Ёе[2]	yo	e		Цц	ts	ts
Жж	zh	zh		Чч	ch	ch
Зз	z	z		Шш	sh	sh
Ии	i	i		Щщ	shch	shch
Йй	y[3]	i[3]		Ъъ	—[4]	″
Кк	k	k		Ыы	y	y
Лл	l	l		Ьь	—[4]	′
Мм	m	m		Ээ	e	e
Нн	n	n		Юю	yu	iu
Оо	o	o		Яя	ya	ia
Пп	p	p				

Combinations of Letters				Equivalents for Old	
	I	II		Style Russian Letters	
				Old Style	New Style
-ый (in names)	-y[5]	-yi		І і	Ии
-ий (in names)	-y[6]	-ii		Ѣ ѣ	Ее
-ия	-ia	-iia		Ѵ ѵ	Ии
-ье	-ie	-′e		Ѳ ѳ	Фф
-ьи	-yi	-′ï			
кс	x	ks		Ъ ъ (terminal)	omitted

System I is used in the text for personal and place names only. System II is used in the text for transliteration of poetry and prose, and for bibliographic entries in the Notes and References section and in the Selected Bibliography section.

---

*Based on J. Thomas Shaw's *The Transliteration of Modern Russian for English-Language Publications,* The University of Wisconsin Press, Madison: 1967.

Notes on Transliteration Table

1. The spelling *Ye-* is not used initially (for example: Evtushenko *not* Yevtushenko).

2. Since pronunciation is emphasized in System I, this letter is transliterated as *yo* (for example: Alyosha).

3. See also Combinations of Letters above.

4. Simply omitted with no indication of omission.

5. Preferred instead of *-i* (for example: Bely).

6. Preferred instead of *-i* for both prenames and surnames (for example: Dmitry *not* Dmitri; Dostoevsky *not* Dostoevski).

CHAPTER 1

Early Writings

I At the Source of Russian Sentimentalism

> On the score of sentimentality, many funny and
> amusing things might be said; but we want to judge
> it, and not mock it. It is an important occurrence
> in man's historical development.
>
> —V. G. Belinsky

EIGHTEENTH-CENTURY Russia experienced a dramatic
growth in the socio-political sphere which is reflected in literature by the trend away from the syllabic poetry and narrative tale of
the seventeenth century. New works were produced by such writers
as Feofan Prokopovich, Antioch D. Kantemir, Vasily K. Trediakovsky, Mikhail V. Lomonosov, and Alexander P. Sumarokov. From
1760 to 1770, many writers appeared on the literary scene, the most
prominent being Alexander N. Radishchev, Denis I. Fonvizin,
Nikolay I. Novikov, Mikhail M. Kheraskov, Mikhail N. Muravyov.
In their works, the tradition of the Enlightenment was carried on and
given a new interpretation in literary Classicism. Of great importance
was the broad knowledge of Western European literature that
Russian writers had—works of the French Enlightenment in
particular.

As in other countries, the Enlightenment in Russia encompassed
a whole epoch and was one of the main stimuli in literary development. Belief in the vast possibilities of the human mind, desire for
knowledge, and a struggle against fanaticism were elements typical
of the Enlightenment and vitally important in the works of the outstanding Russian writers of the eighteenth century. In Russia, the
Age of Enlightenment coincided with a period of accelerated growth
in literature, and certain specific features of the Russian Enlightenment were linked with social and political conditions in Russia,
such as economic backwardness, serfdom, and an absolute autocracy. Russian enlighteners gave more than usual attention to
state organization: they saw that "the only possible means of

bettering the life of society [was] in the spreading of education [and] the propagation of knowledge." As a result, there would be gradual changes—"reforms in all elements of the social and economic structure and in state laws."[1] Concomitantly, the question of education and upbringing, ever the center of attention of Russian men of letters of the eighteenth century, became a matter of growing urgency.

Like its European counterpart, Russian Enlightenment was not uniform: its development was marked by several stages, each consisting of different trends and divisions within the movement. In addition, there were other trends having some points of contact with the Enlightenment, but not fully within its periphery. This accounts for associating with the Age of Enlightenment works of writers who had little in common in their views and styles. By the 1760's, the ideas of the Enlightenment had become so widespread in Russia that political leaders could not ignore them any longer.

Ascending the throne in 1762, Catherine the Great quickly realized how important it was to gain a reputation as an enlightened sovereign in order to turn public opinion in her favor. She corresponded with outstanding European philosophers and writers, wrote literary works herself, took part in the affairs of the Academy of Sciences, and showed an interest in educational problems. But all her efforts were one-sided and superficial. The lofty ideas of the Empress remained unimplemented. In reality, the fate of thousands of people depended on the whims of the Empress' favorites who were frequently dropped and replaced by others. Backbreaking toil, poverty, hunger, fear, and ignorance were the lot of most Russian peasants. The Pugachyov uprising of 1773 to 1776 pointed up serious shortcomings in Catherine's policies. Most intellectuals and the educated class became increasingly convinced that the Empress was far from being an ideal enlightened ruler and that the government was in no position to meet the material and spiritual needs of society. During this period the *Weltanschauung* of A. N. Radishchev was formed, and in 1790 he published his revolutionary book *Journey from Petersburg to Moscow*. Although Radishchev's ideas were alien to most of the nobility, a feeling of dissatisfaction and skepticism was increasingly taking hold in the minds of public figures and men of letters.

One form of reaction to the policies of Catherine the Great was Freemasonry—with its complex and conflicting ideology, philosophy, and culture. Having become widely spread in Russia by the end of the 1770's and the beginning of the 1780's, Freemasonry embraced many different currents, the most important of which was linked with the Enlightenment and which played a significant role in the history of Russian culture. The activities of Novikov and his friends—among them Johann S. Schwartz, Alexey M. Kutuzov, Ivan P. Turgenev, and Alexander A. Petrov, who founded *Druzheskoe uchyonoe obshchestvo* (The Friendly Learned Society) in Moscow in the late 1770's—were directly connected with Freemasonry.

They were far from being unanimous in their views, but many points united them, above all, the desire to be useful to their countrymen. A typical example is their announcement for subscriptions to *Utrenniy svet* (*Morning Light*), a journal which Novikov and his friends began publishing in 1777. Part of the announcement reads as follows: "Since public benefit, moral conduct, and enlightenment are the publishers' chief aims, the said publishers have made it a firm rule to insert in these pages only matter which serves true enlightenment." [2] In the same announcement the publishers informed the public that the money received from subscriptions to the journal would be used to found schools for children of the poor and for orphans, as well as homes for old people. This was one of the most successful ventures of Novikov's Society and quite typical of all its activities.

Particularly important was Novikov's role as publisher and head of the Typographical Company, established in Moscow in 1784, whose board was comprised of members of the Friendly Learned Society. Books published by Novikov made up a large portion of the total book production in Russia. In 1788, of 336 works published in Russia, 155—that is, 41 percent—came off Novikov's printing press. Thus, the Masonic group gathered around Novikov exerted a strong influence on Russian intellectual life, and this influence was just as varied as the views of the Masons themselves. [3]

The works Novikov published were diverse: books on science and history, fiction by Russian authors, and translations of foreign works, including numerous books by eminent Western European authors of the Enlightenment such as Rousseau and Voltaire. There were also books of a mystical character, reflecting the Masons' interest in occultism and cabalism in their search for the "true" religion. At the end of the 1770's and the beginning of the 1880's, signs of conflicting philosophical and esthetic teachings were evident in Novikov's journals, the *Morning Light* (1777–80), *The Moscow Monthly* (1781), and the *Evening Light* (1782).

Even though they were dissimilar from a literary point of view, these journals were clearly connected with Sentimentalism. The Masons attached great importance to man's self-knowledge and self-perfection, and were therefore attracted by works which described emotional experiences, intricate transitions from one mood to another, alternating feelings, and the resulting inner conflicts. A. M. Kutuzov, one of the most active members of Novikov's circle, a "sympathizer" and friend of Radishchev, translated into Russian the moralizings of Christian Fürchtegott Gellert, Heinrich Berische's *Travels of Virtue*—an imitation of Laurence Sterne's *Sentimental Journey*—and Edward Young's *Night Thoughts.*[4] Increased Russian interest in European Sentimentalism and pre-Romanticism almost coincides with a similar phenomenon in American literature from 1770 to 1790, as evidenced by the works of the poet Philip Freneau, the novelist Susanna Rowson, and other American authors.

The tendency of Russian Masons to analyze their own feelings is particularly noticeable in their letters. European epistolary fiction (*The New Heloïse, Werther*) often served as examples for unconscious imitation. This was particularly true of those who shared the credo formulated by one of the leading figures of Russian Freemasonry in 1776: "What I feel, that is my law."[5] Letter-writing grew into a special literary genre, flexible enough to give full play to the expression of abstract moral reflections, yet descriptive of the writer's personal experiences and moods. As a rule, these letters were not intended for publication and, among those that could be classed as original prose writings, comparatively few were fully typical of Sentimentalism.

Meanwhile, new literary tendencies appeared more frequently in the works of poets connected with the Masonic movement: Kheraskov in the 1760's, and later Muravyov. For instance, the "philosophical" odes of Kheraskov differed greatly from those of Russian Classicism in that they elaborated on themes and motifs which had previously appeared in the lyrics of Sumarokov: thoughts about the transience of life, the vanity of all things, an appeal to be satisfied with little, and aspiration toward virtue. All were "the result of a reappraisal of social and moral values taking place in the depths of Classicism."[6] However, Kheraskov's lyrics had not yet become a poetry of the emotions: his odes were far too rational, too full of abstract reflections with little of the individual or personal.

The changes taking place in the *Weltanschauung* of Russian men of letters of the eighteenth century are even more noticeable in the works of M. N. Muravyov, who was the immediate precursor of writers of the 1790's and the following decade—the years closely linked with Karamzin.[7] Muravyov's lyrics gradually grew into a regular cult of feelings, and consequently, "sensitivity of the soul" was already looked upon as the hallmark of a true poet. He called himself "the sage of the single moment," because he felt that everything around was precarious and insecure. In the literature of Classicism, the concept of time had only a primary meaning, and Muravyov was one of the first to reach the new revelation of a world where everything was in constant flux, impermanent, and where "each moment had its special color."[8]

Themes previously met in Kheraskov's writings take on a new freshness in Muravyov's: philosophical motifs come naturally into his poetry, so varied in genre. His poetry was no longer the pure ode, but epistles and light verse. Even Muravyov's style changed accordingly, as did his approach to language which had to express above all the author's mood and his inner state of mind.

The new tendencies appearing in Russian literature during the 1770's and 1780's did not make a clear-cut and definite impact. Nevertheless, all the prerequisites necessary for the growth of Russian Sentimentalism were present, though it had not yet become a separate literary trend. This vague tendency was to be crystallized in the works of Karamzin, which were being formed during this period when all the specific signs and traits of Sentimentalism were present, but in a haphazard form. Literary talent alone did not make Karamzin the leader of the new trend; he reached preeminence also through having spent his early years among people of education—philosophers and men of letters who were in the center of the Masonic movement.

II   *The Shaping of Karamzin's Literary Interests*

> Anything pleasant to read exerts an influence on the
> mind; lacking this, neither can the heart feel nor the
> imagination conceive.
>
> —N. M. Karamzin

Nikolay Mikhaylovich Karamzin was born on December 1
(December 12th, Old Style), 1766, not far from the town of Simbirsk
(now Ulyanovsk) into the family of a comparatively poor member
of the nobility, a retired officer. His relatives and their friends bore
no resemblance to the ignorant landed gentry whom Denis I.
Fonvizin depicted in his comedy *Nedorosl'* (*The Minor*) which
faithfully mirrored the coarse mode of life led by the Russian
provincial gentry of those times. Karamzin learned to read in early
childhood and by the time he was eight or nine, he was already rather
well-read. He perused with delight the legendary story of Roland
through the translation of the well-known Russian writer Vasily
K. Trediakovsky and also translations of novels and other books
he discovered in the family library.

Karamzin's education took on a more formal character when he
was sent in 1780 to the boarding school of Johannes M. Schaden,
a professor at Moscow University. After successfully studying
foreign languages there for a few years, the boy mastered German
particularly well and, in line with the interests of Schaden himself,
found time to get acquainted with German literature. As Karamzin
recalled later, Schaden taught morals from the lectures of Christian
Fürchtegott Gellert.

The education Karamzin received at Schaden's *pension* and certain
lectures he attended at Moscow University gave him a solid basis
for his later literary pursuits. No less important for the future writer
was his continual association with well-educated people who took
a lively interest in literature. In 1783, during his stay in St. Petersburg,
he became acquainted with the poet Ivan Ivanovich Dmitriev, who
later recalled his early friendship with Karamzin in these words: "We
were practically inseparable for almost a year: our predilection for
literature, perhaps even a similarity in our moral makeup, strengthened our ties every day. We told one another what books we had
read: incidentally, I sometimes showed him my little translations

which were published separately, as well as in the journals of those days. Following my example, he also began translating."[9] This friendship, which benefited both, deepened with the years and lasted to the day Karamzin died. He looked on Dmitriev as his main authority in the sphere of poetry. In letters to his friend, the young Karamzin often included verses on themes relating to events or moods mentioned in their correspondence. These were verses dedicated to a special occasion, although not an official one, as in the poetry of Classicism (accession to the throne, birthday of the Empress, etc.). They concerned only the personal lives of the two friends.

In 1783, Karamzin's first publication came out: a translation of Gessner's idyll *Derevyannaya noga* (*The Wooden Leg—Das Hölzerne Bein*). The choice in itself was typical of the times. The name of Salomon Gessner was well known in Russia. His works were frequently translated during the eighteenth century, some of them several times. The "idyll" tells the following story:

A young shepherd meets an old man with a wooden leg who is going up into the mountains. The young shepherd brings water from a stream for the old man who relates how he lost his leg in battle: a soldier had saved his life, but he had been unable to find his rescuer later. It turns out that the soldier was the young shepherd's father, now dead. Happy at the encounter, the old man invites his young acquaintance home and introduces him to his beautiful daughter who gladly agrees to marry the shepherd. A rather lengthy part of the idyll is devoted to a description of the battle in which the Swiss are shown as heroic fighters, ready "to do or die" to uphold their independence. Later, the theme of a "free Switzerland" is further elaborated in Karamzin's works.[10]

While translating Gessner's idyll into Russian, the sixteen-year-old Karamzin was filled with youthful dreams of military feats of glory. In the Russia of that time, people of high birth were registered in the army from childhood; thus, Karamzin already bore the rank of junior ensign (second lieutenant). Now he felt the desire to serve actively in the regular army, but his dream remained unfulfilled because of material difficulties, since noblemen had to have considerable financial means at their disposal on entering military service.

When his father died at the end of 1783, Karamzin sent in his resignation refusing a commission and returned to Simbirsk, where he lived for a short time. But soon he left for Moscow on the advice of a prominent Mason, Ivan Petrovich Turgenev, whose attention was drawn to the talented young man. Turgenev introduced him to Nikolay I. Novikov's circle where, in Dmitriev's words, "Karamzin's education was begun, not only as an author, but in moral training." So the young Karamzin became acquainted with Novikov, A. M. Kutuzov, and other members of the Friendly Learned Society.

He came to be especially close to Alexander Andreevich Petrov, an unusual and highly educated man. Petrov published only translations, but the type of works he chose to translate and his letters— still extant—give an idea of his personal views. A participant in the endeavors of Novikov's circle, Petrov was in many respects an exception among the Masons. The propagation of Christian humility, the conviction that life should be dedicated to preparing oneself for death—so characteristic of certain mystically minded members of the Friendly Learned Society—were ideas absolutely alien to Petrov, who was more inclined to be a skeptic and rationalist.

Personal contact with Petrov proved extremely valuable to Karamzin, helping him overcome a certain artificiality and unnaturalness that involuntarily crept into the sensitive outpourings of this fervid young man. Karamzin was a few years younger than Petrov and he highly respected the opinion of his older friend who knew literature well, had mastered several foreign languages, and had a subtle esthetic taste. With either an ironical remark or a joke, Petrov would induce Karamzin to take a new look at things which he had previously viewed from only one aspect. For example, Petrov managed to change Karamzin's prejudice against rural life. This problem, discussed in their correspondence, was given a very broad application. The points that concerned them were the perception of nature and the principles of expressing reality in literature. Petrov's opinion on this question was based on his profound understanding of Western European literary experiments and the esthetic ideas of the eighteenth century. He wrote Karamzin: "Simplicity of feeling is higher than any other subtlety of thought: it's a sin to belittle nature—a genius—with pedantic imitations and farfetched spurious ideas of low minds. However, simplicity is not a matter of either real or feigned ignorance."[11] In addition, Petrov pointed out the need for observing the rules in poetry, citing Fénelon, Addison, and Gellert, who retained simplicity but followed the rules.

Petrov took a lively interest in all Karamzin's pursuits: his reading, his translations, and his letters to Johann K. Lavater, the Swiss writer, philosopher, and physiognomist. This correspondence is worthy of attention, for it reveals Karamzin's range of interests as a youth and, in addition, is one of the most extensive manuscripts from his early years. Like his older Masonic friends, Karamzin strove to give his letters literary form, to build them into a personal, stylized literary genre. This tendency, which later was given full rein in his *Letters of a Russian Traveller*, was apparent even in his correspondence with Lavater. They wrote to one another in German, and Karamzin showed how brilliantly he knew the language. As time went on (1786–90) the style of Karamzin's letters changed, but at first they were enthusiastic, rather long, too full of dots and dashes, exclamation points, and rhetorical questions.

Karamzin plies Lavater with questions on subjects constantly discussed in Novikov's circle: Is there any proof of the immortality of the soul? What is the bond between body and soul? What is the aim of human existence? Karamzin's interest in these questions was doubtless conceived and encouraged to grow under the influence of his association with the Masons. However, the answers supplied by his older friends failed to satisfy, as he himself admitted in one of his letters. From Lavater he expected more palatable explanations to the question that excited him, for Lavater was a philosopher who "studied people." However naïve physiognomy might have been scientifically, it was one of the first attempts at creating a science dealing with human psychology. This above all was what attracted Karamzin, who was resolved to penetrate the mysteries of man's inner world. The meaning of true happiness was for Karamzin a question inseparable from that of self-knowledge.

Eager to explore the complex problems of human existence, Karamzin read Gellert, Albrecht von Haller, Charles Bonnet, and other moralist writers and philosophers. He took part in the translation section of Novikov's circle, translating von Haller's poem *Vom Ursprung des Übels,* 1734 (*On the Origin of Evil*) and excerpts from German works: *Reflections on the Works of God in the Kingdom of Nature and Providence* and *Conversations with God* (1786), as well as certain other works of Christoph Christian Sturm. However, Karamzin was not drawn to religious and mystical works. He showed greater interest in literature of a worldly character and was encouraged in this by his association with Dmitriev and Petrov.

As early as 1785, Karamzin and Petrov were writing one another about Shakespeare and Voltaire's unjust criticism of him. Petrov knew English, read Shakespeare in the original, and apparently succeeded in arousing Karamzin's interest in the English language and in English literature. His interest grew under the influence of the German poet Jacob M. R. Lenz who was in Moscow at that time. Lenz, one of the stormy geniuses of the *Sturm und Drang*, was an enthusiastic admirer of Shakespeare's genius and in his *Anmerkungen übers Theatre,* 1774 (*Theatre Notes*) promoted the idea of Shakespeare's superiority over Voltaire, dwelling in detail on *Julius Caesar*. Undoubtedly Lenz's work drew the attention of the young Karamzin to *Julius Caesar*.[12] Not suprisingly, therefore, the publications of the Typographical Company for 1787 included Karamzin's translation of *Julius Caesar, a Tragedy by William Shakespeare*.

This was one of the very first Russian translations of Shakespeare, and its preface gave the reader a general idea of the works of the great playwright and their importance. Karamzin wrote the preface himself—his first experimental essay in the historical-critical literary genre.

Pointing out that the Russian reader was "completely unacquainted" with English literature, Karamzin launches directly into a description of Shakespeare as a "great man" and a "genius." Above all he values Shakespeare for his ability "to fathom human nature." "There are few," wrote Karamzin, "who know so well as this amazing word-painter all the secret springs of man, his innermost motives, or the distinctive nuances of every passion, every temperament, and every sphere of life."[13] He quotes the opinion of Voltaire, who accused Shakespeare of not observing the principles of fine literature, which Voltaire deemed obligatory, but Karamzin disagrees with Voltaire, saying that Shakespeare is above judgment, because his genius—like nature itself—could never be bound by any set regulations.

Though Karamzin was still not too well informed on all the critical arguments then raging around Shakespeare's works in European literature, he was able to set down a well-composed and clearly defined picture of what he did know and, even more important, to express his own personal approach to Shakespeare. Karamzin's preface was designed to awaken the interest of Russian readers not only toward Shakespeare but English literature in general, and he called Edward Young and James Thomson the best English writers.

Karamzin's preface also expresses his views on problems of translation: the translator must aim at maximum exactness, should not change the author's ideas, and yet at the same time avoid expressions foreign to the native language. Karamzin, however, coped rather well with his complicated task, and on the whole, much of the dialogue was translated into lively, expressive Russian.

Translating a Shakespearean drama proved an excellent exercise for the budding writer. He acquired good practice that also helped develop his artistic taste. His translation of *Julius Caesar* was the first step which led him away from purely Masonic endeavors. Karamzin received unfailing sympathy and support from Petrov, who looked on literature as an art and not merely a means of education.

In one of his letters, written in 1787, Petrov drew Karamzin's attention to a play by Gotthold Ephraim Lessing, *Emilia Galotti*, remarking that he liked it even more than Shakespeare's tragedies. The following year Karamzin's translation of this work came out. In the short preface Karamzin informed his readers that he had translated Lessing's tragedy "for a theatrical production" and, as speed had been essential, "he had been unable to introduce corrections." Dissatisfied with his work, Karamzin began correcting the translation, and only when this was done did he republish it. The preface doubled as a dedication and was addressed "To People who, knowing the true beauty of the drama, love Lessing's tragedies," and he described Lessing as a "philosopher whose gaze pierces the very heart of mankind."[14] A Russian translation of *Emilia Galotti* had already been published in St. Petersburg in 1784, so Karamzin showed a certain daring when he decided to do a new translation. His book did turn out to be a success, and Lessing's play in Karamzin's translation was staged at the Moscow Theater.

III *Contributor to the* Readings for Children

> The public liked the *Readings for Children* with its novel topics and diverse material, despite the rather crude translation of many plays.
>
> —N. M. Karamzin

The journal *Detskoe chtenie dlya serdtsa i razuma (Readings for Children)*, which Novikov began publishing in 1785, was the natural follow-up to his former activities as a publisher of pedagogical materials. Novikov realized that a lack of children's literature in Russian was seriously hampering the cause of education, and *Readings for Children* was the first Russian periodical especially intended for the young.[15] It carried articles in a readable form on physics, history, and geography, as well as selections that were morally educational: amusing and instructive stories, fables, and so on. For the most part, they were translations, usually from the German.

Petrov took an active part in the journal's publication, and soon Karamzin began contributing. Gradually, these two writers assumed editorial responsibility for the journal, though from 1787 until its termination in 1789, Karamzin was the principal and almost sole contributor. Much space in the journal was devoted to Karamzin's translation of *Les Veillées du château* (1784) by Madame Stéphanie Félicité de Genlis *(Derevenskie vechera)*, a cycle of short tales.

Mme de Genlis' characters were not only people of noble birth, but also simple peasants endowed with high moral qualities. The French writer was attracted by features which speak of man's emotional sensitivity, irrespective of his social standing. Her short tales were candidly sermonizing: good is rewarded, evil is punished. Despite all the naïveté of her ethics, Karamzin found much in her works of interest to himself and to the Russian reading public, above all, the emphasis on the psychology of the main characters. In his own works later on, Karamzin made use of several motifs from de Genlis' works which he knew so well. The very fact that Karamzin turned to the short tales of de Genlis is also significant, as it marks his first break with German literature. Working on the *Readings for Children*, the writer tried to give his readers a wide selection, acquainting them not only with German literature—the translation of Christian Weisse's poem *Arkadsky pamyatnik* (*The Arcadian Monument*), among others—but with French and English.

From among English writers, Karamzin chose James Thomson, with translated prose versions of "Spring," "Summer," "Autumn," and "Winter," from the poem *The Seasons* (1726–30), followed by its closing *Hymn* which he put into verse form. Karamzin's admiration for Thomson is apparent in one of his first original prose pieces *Progulka* (*A Stroll*) published in *Readings for Children*.

The sketch has no plot; it merely describes the changing moods of its hero when he takes a stroll in the country on a spring night. He watches the setting sun from a river bank, "wrapped in meditation and in his sensations." With the coming of darkness he becomes acutely aware of being alive: "I feel keenly that I am alive, that I am something separate from others, that I am an absolute entity."[16] But almost at once the hero's mood is clouded by the thought of nonexistence, of death. The rising of the moon draws him out of these reflections and he recalls Young, whose name he associates with the moonlit landscape, and afterwards Homer, Ossian, Wieland. He hears a nightingale singing and falls asleep. Awakening at dawn, he watches the sun come up, then on his way back to town, reads Thomson's *Hymn* in the book he had taken with him.

There is very little originality in this prose sketch. The author himself mentions Young and Thomson, whose influence on his work is more than apparent. However, Karamzin's *A Stroll* was one of the first attempts in Russian literature at writing lyrical prose, and, in spite of being imitative, it undoubtedly reflected moods sincerely felt by the young Russian author at the time.

Thomson's name is also found in Karamzin's poem *Poetry*, which is rightly considered his conspectus of this art; it sums up his ideas on the purpose of poetry:

> In every, every country, Poetry enhallowed
> Was preceptress of the people, and happiness bestowed;
> For all hearts everywhere with love she warmed and mellowed.[17]

Karamzin tells in detail what he thinks true poetry is, what is typical of certain authors, from the biblical David to the legendary Orpheus of Greek mythology. Among authors of antiquity he mentions Homer, Sophocles, Euripides, Bion, Theocritus, Moschus, Horace, and Ovid. Karamzin was anxious to stress the impact of poetry on human beings:

> When Homer starts to sing
> All are warriors, all heroes; when Theocritus—
> They lay down arms—and shepherds now they all become!
> All hearts and feelings bow to Poetry as subjects.

> (*CPW*, p. 60)

For Karamzin, "Britain is the mother of the greatest poets," and his translations of English writers occupy a place of importance in his poetical works: James Macpherson's *Songs of Selma*, which were allegedly composed by the ancient Irish bard, Ossian; as well as Shakespeare, Milton, Young, and Thomson. He continues to speak of Shakespeare in almost the same vein as he did in the foreword to his translation of *Julius Caesar*: Shakespeare "understood people's hearts" and "had found the key to all the great secrets of Fate." To Karamzin, he was "a great man," "an immortal mind." The young poet saw a "lofty spirit" in the works of Milton; he spoke of Young as "a friend of the unfortunate, comforter of the miserable." He is grateful to Thomson for teaching him "to delight in Nature." From German authors, Karamzin singles out Gessner and Klopstock, author of the poem *Messias*, translated into Russian by A. M. Kutuzov. In Karamzin's eyes, Friedrich Gottlieb Klopstock is a "chosen singer," a poet initiated into the divine mysteries. It is significant that Karamzin chose the epigraph to his poem *Poetry* from Klopstock: "Die Lieder der göttlichen Harfenspieler schallen mit Macht, wie beseelend."[18] These words agree with the main idea of the poem of Karamzin's, which affirms poetry as the highest manifestation of the human spirit. Russian writers are not mentioned in the poem; however, there are lines which have aroused various conjectures among literary critics:

> O Russians! Comes the age when also in your midst
> Such poetry will start to shine, as does the noonday sun;
> Night gloom has vanished, even now Aurora's light
> In **** is gleaming; and soon all nations of the world
> Will northward flow in pilgrimage to light their lamps.

(CPW, p. 63)

Some consider the omitted word, marked by four asterisks, to be the name of Karamzin himself. But the more convincing argument comes from critics who believe that Karamzin had Kheraskov or Derzhavin in mind.[19]

In later years Karamzin was rather critical of his early poetical works and left many out of his collections. He was also critical of his prose, and from many collections he omitted the short tale *Evgeniy i Yulia* (*Eugene and Julia*), published in the *Readings for Children*. However, this tale is of some interest, if only because it is one of the most important early works of the budding writer.

Eugene and Julia was subtitled *A True Russian Tale*. In eighteenth-century literature, the tendency to stress the truth of the events depicted was a long-standing habit. Gradually a specific genre was formed—the "genuine," the "true" or "half-true" short tale (*povest*). It was also very important to indicate that this tale was purely Russian in origin, since most other works published then were translations, although the author and language of the original story were scarcely ever mentioned. The narrative or Karamzin's tale is very simple, and belongs to "the sad event" type if one accepts the classification given by Peter Brang.[20]

Mrs. L. lives in the country with her ward Julia and awaits the arrival of her son Eugene, who is studying "in foreign lands." Eugene arrives home, and his old friendship with Julia grows into a love, which is mutual. Mrs. L. confesses that she "prepared them for each other" and gives their future union her blessing. However, Eugene suddenly falls ill and dies, leaving Mrs. L. and Julia to "life-long melancholy solitude."

Karamzin's characters are cardboard figures, lacking individuality, but most important is the fact that they are "sensitive." In this light the subtitle acquires greater significance: in the author's opinion, it was quite unnecessary to turn exclusively to foreign novels to find "sensitivity," for this was something inherent even in people living right near Moscow. Readers could meet them and become just as "sensitive" themselves. In the description of how Mrs. L., Julia, or Eugene spent their time, there is not the faintest clue to the actual, everyday life of a Russian family of good birth. Karamzin's characters are idyllic stereotypes: in summer they go for strolls, admiring sunrise or sunset or a flock of "gentle sheep" while the shepherd plays his pipes of Pan. Karamzin introduces an incident Gessner used in his *Wooden Leg*, which Karamzin had translated: Mrs. L. recalls how Eugene once brought a drink of water to a tired old man, thus showing "signs of a sensitive heart." However, the tragic outcome of the tale has nothing to do with an idyll and even contradicts it. In an idyll the noble-hearted heroes are rewarded for virtue and enjoy happiness, but in Karamzin's tale the opposite is true. The climax in the plot comes at the very moment the reader expects a description of the happy marriage of the two lovers. On the eve of their marriage, Mrs. L. is pouring out her heart in prayer, and "one is led to think," writes Karamzin, "that these heartfelt entreaties will bring the young couple a happy ending." "But the ways of the Almighty are mysteries beyond human comprehension,"[21] he continues, preparing the reader for what is to follow.

Thus, in this tale, though it is artistically of little interest, one can trace a theme very essential in Karamzin's writings of later years— the theme of fate. It also reveals the writer's attraction to psychological problems, though his grasp of them is somewhat naïve. Karamzin's characters experience a sharp reversal of attitude toward the world with a change in their inner feelings when they are suddenly dropped from perfect bliss into hopelessness and despair. They look upon the world with new eyes: "Nature itself, once a source of joy, has now become gloomy and desolate."[22] Similar contrasts are later encountered in a great number of Karamzin's works.

In comparison with Karamzin's earlier translations, where his language was considerably freighted with Old Church Slavonic words, *Eugene and Julia* is written in a simple, flowing style. Earlier, especially in his translations from German where he was under the influence of German syntax, Karamzin often used clumsy and complex constructions. But gradually his style became more fluent and natural, and in his own compositions he could permit himself greater freedom, no longer hemmed in by the text of another author. As a result, Karamzin's language developed more flexibility: the repetition of balanced constructions and individual words gave a special resonance and a unique rhythmic pattern to Karamzin's prose. One example is the following passage from *Eugene and Julia*: "They took longer walks than usual; they lingered over their dinner, lingered over their evening meal; one confident her son would come, the other confident her brother would."[23] This attention to euphony of language, which was developed early in Karamzin thanks to his poetical bent, is also evident in his later prose.[24]

CHAPTER 2

Moscow Journal

I *Impudent Venture*

> In the *Moscow Journal* Karamzin has razed the Gothic
> towers of decaying literature, and on the ashes has
> started a new European publication which awaits
> skillful and diligent hands to bring it to perfection.
> —P. A. Vyazemsky

IN the autumn of 1790, Karamzin returned to Moscow after travelling a year and a half through Europe, visiting Germany, Switzerland, France, and England, and meeting prominent writers and
philosophers. Travelling enriched his mind with new impressions and
gave the final touch to his education. Karamzin's vague dreams of a
literary career now shaped themselves into a clear, definite goal.
He decided to become a publisher himself. In November 1790, he
announced in *Moskovskie vedomosti* (*Moscow News*) that beginning
in January 1791, he would be publishing the *Moskovsky zhurnal*
(*Moscow Journal*).

Describing the tentative plans for the journal, the budding publisher pointed out that printing "only theological, mystical, over-
scholarly, and pedantic dry pieces did not fit into" his plans.[1]
Naturally, such an announcement put many of Karamzin's Masonic
friends on the alert. This venture of the young writer, who ostenta-
tiously refused to feature mystical literary works in his publication,
seemed to them inexcusable impudence, although the Masons were
not unanimous in this attitude toward Karamzin's project.

A. M. Kutuzov declared that Karamzin's announcement had
"dealt a blow to his heart." Wishing to divert the young man from
his purpose, Kutuzov went so far as to write a lampoon: it pointedly
told about a presumptuous young author, named "Parrot Monkey,"
who "firmly decided to write, though he himself did not quite
know—what!"[2] There are grounds for suggesting that Kutuzov
felt a certain alarm for the budding publisher, because a friend of
his, the writer Alexander Radishchev, had been arrested that same

year (in 1790), and the government's suspicious attitude toward the activities of Novikov's circle was already evident. At the same time Kutuzov saw Karamzin's project as a vain desire for fame and condemned it.

Other Masons, not on a friendly footing with Karamzin, took an even sharper and more hostile attitude toward the *Moscow Journal*. For example, M. I. Bagryansky wrote the following to Kutuzov about the young publisher: "Il donne au public un journal, le plus mauvais sans doute qu'on peut présenter au monde éclairé. Il croit nous enseigner des choses, que nous n'avons jamais connues."[3] Karamzin's venture was similarly viewed by Nikolay N. Trubetskoy, who also considered that the economic difficulties connected with the journal's publication were a deserved punishment for the young man's impudence.

Many were particularly surprised and indignant when Kheraskov began contributing to the *Moscow Journal*, for he was a Mason and was already a venerable writer held in great esteem by Novikov's circle. His poem *The Times* opened the first issue of the *Moscow Journal*—a matter of great importance for Karamzin.

A few other Masons regarded Karamzin's venture with understanding: D. I. Dmitrievsky, Ivan P. Turgenev, Fyodor N. Klyucharev were contributors to the magazine, and—of course—Alexander A. Petrov who had previously encouraged Karamzin's interest in literature other than that of a mystical nature.

Of special importance was the support the young publisher received from his close friends, the Mason Alexey Alexandrovich Pleshcheev and his wife Anastasia Ivanovna, with whom Karamzin stayed after returning from abroad. Even so, Mme. Pleshcheeva, for whom Karamzin had retained a tender affection over the years, wrote uneasily to Kutuzov about the change in Karamzin after his tour: "He has stayed with us since he came back, but I see much in him that I should prefer not to . . . . I clearly realize that he is completely different and, worst of all, he himself believes he is better now than he was . . . . The change in him is also this: he has become more self-reliant, as you once foretold."[4]

Grounds for concern really did exist: revolutionary events in France in 1789 aroused a lively response in Russia. Fear of the "French infection" increased Catherine's suspicious attitude toward any association that strove to be independent of her, especially toward the Masons, who had close ties with the Tsarevich Paul, now of age and the lawful claimant to the throne. From 1790 the authorities placed the members of the Novikov circle under careful surveillance and their letters were subject to "scrutiny and copying." The Masons, feeling their situation was growing more and more dangerous, tried to be as guarded as possible. In their correspondence they frequently mentioned their loyalty to the Empress and expressed indignation at the French revolution.

All the same, Karamzin—who, before his trip abroad, had been closely associated with the Masons and was privy to many affairs of Novikov's circle—began to show great independence. Naturally, under the new circumstances the Masons could expect additional unpleasant consequences to follow as a result of Karamzin's statement in the press.

Replying to Pleshcheeva, Kutuzov wrote: "Evidently the tour wrought a great change in him, in the eyes of his former friends. Perhaps, inwardly, he underwent a sort of French Revolution."[5] Kutuzov was disturbed because after touring Europe, Karamzin took a more critical stand in regard to ideas considered of great importance in Masonic circles. For example, the doctrine of the immortality of the soul and the Masonic views linked with it on man's mission and the meaning of life (earthly life as a temporary stage, a preparation for eternal life after death) now aroused serious doubts in Karamzin. Apropos of Karamzin's words, "I shall love you eternally, if my soul is immortal," Pleshcheeva wrote to Kutuzov: "Just imagine what he is like, if he doubts it! This 'if' is driving me mad!"[6]

Travelling on his own through Europe and meeting many different types of people changed Karamzin's attitude to the Masonic doctrine and, naturally, to the Masons themselves. While his sincere and close friendship with Petrov continued despite their separation during the tour and the change in Karamzin, his relations with the Pleshcheevs were more complicated. Anastasia Ivanovna, who had taken an active part in Karamzin's pursuits and had greatly influenced the young man earlier, felt that the long separation had changed Karamzin and also the character of their relationship. However, she attentively followed the young publisher's venture and saw to it that Kutuzov received the *Moscow Journal*. It was most likely due to the Pleshcheevs that Kutuzov gradually changed his opinion about Karamzin's activities as a publisher. At any rate, in April 1792, he wrote to Anastasia Ivanovna about Karamzin:

"I am somewhat angry with him for not sending me his journal; even if he did not do so the first year, he should not forget me this year at least." [7]

Karamzin had made a magnificent project of his journal, and it had turned out to be a real success. In his earlier "Announcement," the publisher had stated that he had more than enough material. He had in mind his own writings, and it was in the *Moscow Journal* that he began publishing his largest work, the richest in content— *Letters of a Russian Traveller*. A large part of each issue of the journal was taken up by the serialized *Letters*. Even so, Karamzin never managed to print all of them in his journal and completed their publication only some years later. However, Karamzin's fame as a "Russian traveller" and as the author of the *Letters* originated strictly from their publication in the *Moscow Journal*. In fact, any notion of the character of the journal and its impact on the public was derived first and foremost from the *Letters*. Other works of Karamzin printed in the same publication are in one way or another usually related to the *Letters*.

Karamzin published a number of tales, vignettes, and poems in this journal. He also featured a regular "Critical Review," and published his translations of works by foreign authors. In the last issue of the first year he reminded his readers that the *Moscow Journal* was a "one man" publication and that he was perfectly aware of all its shortcomings. Nonetheless, he did succeed in attracting a rather large number of contributors, including established writers. Particularly important was his contact with Gavriil R. Derzhavin, renowned author of the ode to Catherine II, "Felitsa" ("Felicity," 1783). In November 1790, when the journal was still in the planning stage, Karamzin wrote the poet: "When you finish your ode *Perfidy*, please remember that I have reserved space for it in my journal." [8] And, indeed, several issues of the *Moscow Journal* open with Derzhavin's poems. As with most other works, Karamzin published Derzhavin's verses without the author's name or referred to them simply as poems by an "anonymous author." In publishing the poem *Chorals Sung During the Fête at the Potyomkin Palace,* the publisher mentioned that he had received it from a "venerable author." [9] Karamzin always gave preference to Derzhavin's poems, even over those of his friends. Or, as he explained to Dmitriev, the August issue carried only one of his poems because "there were rather many of Derzhavin's." [10]

Derzhavin highly appreciated the literary writings of Karamzin and wrote a poem for the *Moscow Journal* called *A Walk in the Tsar's Village* which concluded with the following lines:

> Nightingale, sing!—even in prose
> Thou art heard, Karamzin![11]

When printing this last line, Karamzin used only his initial and asterisks, but readers could easily guess who was meant.

Dmitriev was not as well known as Derzhavin, but his fame stemmed from his contributions to the *Moscow Journal*. He was the most active contributor to Karamzin's publication.[12] Dmitriev's verses, quite varied in genre, included numerous *bezdelki* ("trifles")—inscriptions, epigrams, ballads, fairy tales, and songs. His song fables won the greatest recognition among his contemporaries, especially those which were literary imitations of folk poetry. A sudden interest in native folklore and the desire to introduce it into literature became an important trend, and Karamzin also published, for example, the authentic text of a Russian folk song, *Uzh kak pal tuman na sine more* (*When Fog Falls O'er the Dark Blue Sea . . .*) which the poet Nikolay A. Lvov passed on to him.

Karamzin's interest in poets of former times is also worthy of attention: he published the translation of an extract from the drama *Sakuntala* by Kalidasa, a famous Hindu writer of the fifth century; also extracts from the *Ossianic poems*, which were taken for authentic works of an ancient Scottish bard, but subsequently proved to be clever forgeries.

Translations of European authors, Karamzin's contemporaries, were also prominently featured: through Jacob Heinrich Meister's work, *Characteristics of German Poets*, the Russian reader gathered some idea of the literary works of Christoph Martin Wieland, Friedrich Gottlieb Klopstock, and Salomon Gessner. Separate works by Wieland, Karl F. Moritz, August Kotzebue, and other German writers were published. From French literature, the publisher chose Jean-François Marmontel, Jean Florian, and the correspondence on philosophy of Pierre Bayle and the Earl of Shaftesbury (Anthony Ashley Cooper).[13] Translations from the English were primarily extracts from Laurence Sterne's *A Sentimental Journey* and *The Life and Opinions of Tristram Shandy, Gentleman*.

The foreign works published in Karamzin's journal were mostly those by authors who were—to one degree or another—associated with European Sentimentalism. But it is interesting that he selected writers who used irony and even skepticism in passages which were supposed to be sentimental (Sterne, Wieland), rather than those whose writings were more idyllic and moralizing (Gessner, Haller).

Karamzin was not content with simply acquainting the Russian public with what he considered the best books in European literature. He also helped form the reader's opinion by regularly expressing his personal views on the works published in his journal. All his notations and forewords form an important addition to the feature section of "Critical Reviews" carried by the *Moscow Journal.*

II *Karamzin the Critic*

But do you really wish there to be no criticism at all?
—N. M. Karamzin

Every issue of the *Moscow Journal* was quite thick—about 400 pages. During the two years it was published, eight issues came out, and, considering that all this work was actually carried out by only one person, it is surprising how Karamzin managed to prepare all the material. In addition, he managed to keep informed on all books published abroad and in Russia, and never missed a new play. The *Moscow Journal* featured Karamzin's literary and theatrical reviews which were not merely informative, but were often short studies revealing the author's esthetic principles.

One of his first reviews was on Kheraskov's novel *Kadm i Garmonia* (*Kadm and Harmonia*), in which Karamzin explained his understanding of poetry. Calling Kheraskov's work sheer poetry, the critic wrote: "The philosopher who is not a poet writes moral dissertations, sometimes rather dry ones; the poet accompanies his moral with fascinating images, makes it come alive through his personages, thus giving it greater impact. He teaches us, so to speak, unobtrusively, feeding our curiosity with a pleasant tale about wonderful things."[14] For Karamzin, poetry was any truly artistic literary work regardless of genre, applied even to prose.

Poetic criteria, for Karamzin, were basic in evaluating and characterizing any literary work. This is evident in his enthusiastic review of the novel *Anna St. Ives* (1792) by the English writer Thomas Holcroft. In the review he says that the author "writes as one inspired, like a poet." But Shakespeare remained Karamzin's measuring stick: "Holcroft's personages are depicted in almost the same way as Shakespeare's."[15]

Karamzin valued every writer by the force of his emotional impact. Reviewing a German novel, he wrote: "Naturally, every reader will be grateful to the author. He knows how to touch the heart, how to fill it with joy or sorrow, and we cannot resist adding either our tears or a smile to those of the author."[16]

From the literary reviews, articles, and notations published in the *Moscow Journal*, Russian Sentimentalism gradually developed its theoretical foundation. Karamzin put his own interpretation on ideas framed by European writers associated with the Sentimentalist trend, showing great independence artistically and a very fine sense of esthetic values. The cult of "sensibility" for him was not an exaltation of the emotions, but an elevation of sensibility to ennobling heights. Karamzin's understanding of "sensibility" was inseparably joined to the Humanist ideas of the times: a "sensitive" person could not be callous, heartless, or cruel to others; he was moved by a stranger's suffering, a stranger's grief, and took them as much to heart as his own. A "sensitive" person, being deeply sympathetic, compassionate, and easily hurt, was quick to respond to everything around him, and the tears coming fast to his eyes were the inevitable outward sign of "sensibility." A "sensitive" person was one specially chosen and blessed with a unique gift, the most valuable gift, according to Sentimentalist views. Endowed with delicate feelings, such a person could see and understand what other people were blind to, did not care about, and considered of little importance.

Whereas the literature of Classicism represented feelings as being indivisibly monolithic, literature now concerned itself with nuances of feelings, with transitions from one mood to another, and with the evolution of sensibility and the dialectics of its development. As one critic states: "Neither Russian nor Western European Sentimentalism could overcome rationalism in esthetics, notwithstanding the cult of 'sensibility' that they had created. But in comparison with Classicism, from which they had inherited the rationalistic concept of an unchangeable human nature, they went deeper into that concept, raising the question about the peculiar manifestation of human nature in the psychology of each individual, and declaring that they understood personality and the significance of personality."[17] Sentimentalists—including Karamzin—became especially interested in the problem of character development, and this question was discussed from every angle in the *Moscow Journal*, specifically, in Karamzin's critical review of a Russian translation of Samuel Richardson's novel *Clarissa Harlow* (1747–48). Karamzin draws the reader's attention to an interesting combination of differing, even contrasting, qualities in the character of Lovelace (sometimes he is noble and kind, sometimes a monster) and affirms that this mixture of good and evil in one character is natural. He carried this view—new for Russian critics—into his own original works when creating some of his characters.

All peoples, no matter what their stage of civilization, were of equal interest to Karamzin both historically and esthetically. The two aspects were closely interwoven in his mind, but as a Sentimentalist writer he searched mainly for signs of "sensibility" in every culture.

Karamzin was also exceedingly attentive to the style and language of translations. He demanded the highest accuracy possible and would ironically object to translating the French word *paysage* ("landscape, scenery") as *zemledelie* ("agriculture") or would point out the incorrect spelling of foreign names in Russian transcription. He considered the stylistic nuances of a word highly important and thought that in transmitting a character's speech, one should find words that suited a particular character and type.

He had similar criteria for the language in translated plays and objected to a heroine using language unsuitable to "her sex and social standing," or to the use of Old Church Slavonic forms typical of the stilted style in a translated comedy. Karamzin felt that "the more natural and simple the language of a play, the better,"[18] and he rejected too much pathos, excessive or unnatural emotion, and misplaced melodrama such as that which occurred in a play where the heroine kisses the dagger before stabbing herself.

Karamzin's views on the theater were expressed more fully in his review of Corneille's *Le Cid*, presented at the Moscow Theater. He begins with a fairly detailed résumé of the tragedy, recalling a production he saw in Paris. He then discusses the changes introduced in the plot by the Russian translator and how the play was received by the French public, citing its many years of success, describing the critical account by the French Academy, and disagreeing with Voltaire's attempted justification of certain weaknesses found in the tragedy. Ending the article with his own critique,

Karamzin writes: "... There are events which are good only for the historian, and not the poet-dramatist. The historian must describe everything as it was, without thinking of the impact the event he is describing may have on the reader; but the poet-dramatist must always keep in mind the special impact he wants to make, that is, he must arouse either joy or grief in the spectator" (*SW*, II, 105–106).

Karamzin thus juxtaposes the historian and the playwright and states that a writer is obliged to observe the specific distinctions of his chosen genre, each genre having its own laws. The point made here, however, is not about different genres, but about dramaturgy in contrast to historical writing. Indirectly, therefore, Karamzin touches upon the question of how a historian should write: he is not allowed to "imagine" but must keep to the facts, describing "everything as it was."

In his review, Karamzin quotes an unfavorable opinion of the play by D'Alembert and agrees with it: most French plays lack "the very horror, the very commiseration that form the very soul of tragedy." In contrast, plays by Shakespeare do possess these qualities, and the Bard of Avon is still the unsurpassable genius to Karamzin, just as he was when Karamzin was translating *Julius Caesar*. Comparing French plays to a "trim, formal garden," Karamzin declares: "In complete contrast, I would liken Shakespeare's works to nature's creations which fascinate us by their very lack of formal planning, and which act on our soul with unspeakable force, marking it with an indelible imprint" (*SW*, II, 107).

Karamzin tried to supply his readers with the most relevant information about the authors and works that he reviewed. In trying to catch the reader's interest, Karamzin—with his personal writing style noted for its exceptional liveliness and facile flow—passes lightly from one theme to another, often interjecting questions in order to draw the reader's attention. For example, in speaking of various faults in Corneille's tragedy, Karamzin suddenly inserts a rhetorical question: "But why, then, did *Le Cid* please French audiences so?" It did, he says, "because it contained really fine scenes and touching emotions; because it had much beautiful poetry" (*SW*, II, 106).

Karamzin's theater reviews were extremely important not only to the general public whom they helped to visualize, understand,

and assess a given play, but also to the actors whom Karamzin
taught how "to approach their roles in order to understand them,
and to see in the personage of a theatrical production a living human
being with all the emotions and sensitive reactions inherently his."[19]

III *Tales*

Oh! I sometimes shed tears and am not ashamed of it!
—N. M. Karamzin

The literary principles set down by Karamzin in his reviews and
critical notes were applied in his other writings. His publications in
the *Moscow Journal* immediately made his name famous, and made
him the recognized leader of Russian Sentimentalism.

His short tale *Bednaya Liza* (*Poor Liza*, 1792) became especially
popular. People of all classes read and admired it. Fashionable
young men and women wept over Karamzin's tale; workers in both
town and country felt sympathy for the fate of the heroine.

The author introduces *Poor Liza* by telling about his walks
around Moscow not far from the Simonov Monastery. All that
meets the author's eye stimulates his reflections and dreams. His
main recollection is linked with a deserted, run-down hut not far
from the monastery walls. This is where poor Liza allegedly lived.
The story begins with a background narrative:

Her father was a well-to-do peasant, but after his death his widow
and daughter fall into want. They rent out their land for a "very
small sum." In the springtime, Liza sells flowers in Moscow. One
time a young man approaches her; he talks tenderly with Liza and
asks her to sell flowers only to him. So begins Liza's acquaintance
with Erast, a wealthy young man of the gentry class. In love with him,
Liza refuses to marry a peasant who has proposed to her. Erast,
though at first sincerely and ardently in love with Liza, gradually
grows cool to her and finally tells her that he must enter military
service. After some time, however, Liza meets Erast by chance and
learns he is going to get married. Leaving him, she is in great despair
and, finding herself on the edge of a pond, throws herself in the water
and drowns. When Erast hears of it, he is tormented by remorse and
remains unhappy to the end of his life.

This tale, in theme and general outline, resembles the moral-laden
Sentimentalist novel *Charlotte, a Tale of Truth* by the American
writer Susanna Rowson, published in England in 1791, the same

year that Karamzin's *Moscow Journal* first came out. Rowson's novel was enormously popular in the United States: from 1794 to 1933, 161 editions were printed, so that it can be considered one of the first American best-sellers. *Poor Liza* was included in all the collections of Karamzin's works published during his lifetime and posthumously. It came out in many separate editions and was included in various prose selections for students.

Both of these fictional works were typical of the times, responding to the demands of the public. Rowson's novel and Karamzin's tale, written quite independently of one another, nevertheless bear a close resemblance to the same type of literature, and even coincide in certain individual details. In *Charlotte,* as in her other works, Rowson stresses that her "tales are founded upon truth."[20] This position was essential in striking an attitude of verisimilitude. Karamzin makes use of a similar device.

The sales announcement of the separate edition of *Poor Liza* published in 1796 described Karamzin's work as "a moving and sensitive historical tale."[21] In those days, "the historical method" meant authenticity, and the tale was accepted as a story of events which had really occurred. Karamzin himself sought to emphasize the truthfulness of the tale: "Why am I not writing a novel, instead of the sad truth?" (*SW,* I, 619) he says, as he relates how Erast told Liza about his marriage. At the end of the tale the author recalls that he became acquainted with Erast one year before the latter's death, heard the story from his own lips, and even went with him to Liza's grave. This type of conclusion strengthened the impression that the events described were absolutely true and permitted the author to give a convincing picture of his personal attitude toward the main characters.

Karamzin is allegedly narrating what he chanced to hear from Erast, who is full of remorse and ready to make the most sincere confession. Liza is shown to the reader as Erast saw her, not as a real peasant girl, but a tender, sensitive "shepherdess." Absolutely no actual details of everyday peasant life are given in the tale, and the images of the peasant women—Liza and her mother—are quite colorless. Their language has little in common with the people's vernacular. For example, Liza's mother speaks of her husband in this manner: "Ah, we never tired of looking at each other up to the very moment cruel death cut him down in his prime. He died in my arms!" (*SW,* I, 614).

Nevertheless, the heroine of Karamzin's tale was a peasant girl, a fact of extraordinary importance in Russian literature. Before this, as a rule, literary works did not depict peasants at all, or else showed them as minor characters who were of little importance. More often than not they were shown as comical figures. Most Classical writers were of the upper class and considered peasants to be rough, primitive, and lacking in the finer feelings.

Sentimentalism, with its cult of sensibility, was based on the idea that man should be valued irrespective of class. Existing long before the appearance of Sentimentalism, this idea had been popular in Russia from the time of Peter the Great. Liberals considered that neither rank nor riches should determine one's judgment of a man, but that the criteria should be his personal abilities. With the Sentimentalists, the idea of personal merit took on a new and different meaning: according to them, man was as great as his power of feeling, regardless of his position in society.

For Karamzin, it was important to confirm the idea that "peasant girls are also capable of loving"—a new and bold idea for the time. "Sensitive" Liza is a peasant girl, and this circumstance adds a particular poignancy to the conflict as a whole. *Poor Liza* differs from most Western-European and American Sentimentalist novels of similar structure due to the motif of social inequality which is the underlying theme of the plot. It is not a matter of Liza being poor and Erast rich, but that she is a peasant and he is a gentleman. The difference in their social standing forms a gulf impossible to bridge according to the views then generally accepted. Therefore, the tragic ending is unavoidable.

It is quite in character that it never occurs to Liza's mother that the "handsome, affectionate *barin*" ("gentleman"), Erast, might marry her daughter. She dreams that Liza will marry a peasant, with Erast standing godfather to their children. Liza herself reminds Erast that he can never be her husband, since she is a peasant. Erast answers this with a passionate outburst: "You've hurt me to the quick! To your friend, to me, the sensitive heart, the innocent soul is more important than anything else—and Liza will always be the one nearest my heart" (*SW*, I, 615). This tirade serves as a natural continuation of the idea that "peasant girls are also capable of loving."

The thoughts of Erast and the author run parallel, so that at times it is difficult to draw a line between them, particularly since the author is retelling the story in Erast's own words. Much of what is told about Erast calls to mind the personal biography of young Karamzin when he lived in Simbirsk before becoming an intimate of the Masons:

This Erast was a fairly rich nobleman with a better than average mind and a kind heart, kind by nature; but [he was] weak and thoughtless. He led a dissipated life, thought only of his own pleasure, sought it in worldly amusements but rarely found it: he was bored and complained of life . . . . He read novels, idylls; he had a rather vivid imagination and often in his thoughts was carried back to the days (whether they had ever existed, or not) when, if you believe the poets, all people wandered carefree through the meadows, bathed in pure springs, kissed like turtledoves, lay at rest among roses and myrtles, and spent all their days in happy idleness. (*SW*, I, 610)

Such moods, typical of a sentimental young man brought up on novels, now stirred Karamzin's full sympathy, yet not without a certain shade of irony. Erast had "a heart kind by nature"; at their first meeting Liza was attracted by his "kind face." If Erast had been in the shoes of the hero of Karamzin's first tale, *Eugene and Julia*, he would have become the same as Eugene—an ideal "sensitive" lover. But Erast's sincere dreams of happiness with his "shepherdess" were impractical, and he became the involuntary cause of her death. As a result, he condemns himself, and his suffering arouses Karamzin's sympathy no less than does Liza's tragic fate. Erast's character, without doubt, is very interesting from a psychological viewpoint. He is certainly not the positive type as is Eugene, but is a combination of conflicting feelings and impulses, a character that goes through a moral evolution.

The social conflict in this tale is not as sharp as the one in Radishchev's *Travel from St. Petersburg to Moscow*. Radishchev draws quite a different picture of a peasant girl, Anyuta, often compared to Karamzin's Liza by literary critics.[22] Karamzin was not concerned merely with the theme of social inequality, but also with the theme of fate, which inevitably makes people bring suffering to others and themselves against their wishes. *Poor Liza* is also one of the author's first attempts to regard his youthful ideals with a critical eye. It brings out quite clearly the irony and skepticism characteristic of Karamzin, the Sentimentalist writer. But very few of Karamzin's admirers and imitators who accepted *Poor Liza* as their manifesto noticed and appreciated this specific peculiarity in the writer's style. Though it brought the writer fame, the tale also provoked many controversial statements against Karamzin, statements which referred to him primarily as the author of *Poor Liza* or, by his own admission, author of "a simple tale."

The neighborhood of the Simonov Monastery, which Karamzin had described, became a place of pilgrimage. The pond where, as the author relates, Liza drowned herself, was given the name "Liza's Pond." In the summer of 1799, when the painter Ivan A. Ivanov was there, he visited the pond and the small hut "which apparently must be the very same one," that is, the dwelling of Liza and her mother. "Now the pond is quite famous," Ivanov continues. "People wander about in droves, reading the inscriptions carved on the trees around the pond. I also read them, but did not find anything worthwhile. Everywhere people are saying that the author lied about Liza drowning herself here, that there never was a Liza. True, some of the inscriptions were written by tenderhearted, sensitive people, who were moved by this pitiful story."[23]

Poor Liza was interpreted in different ways: For some, the important issue was whether the event described was really true; for others, the "tenderhearted" ones—Ivanov included—the vicinity of the Simonov Monastery was "a place enchanted by the wizardry of Karamzin's pen." Consequently, *Poor Liza* was long the subject of controversy, some speaking of it with admiration, others with disparagement. Needless to say, all this added to its popularity.

Other tales by Karamzin published in the *Moscow Journal* are in some ways more interesting than *Poor Liza*. Heading the list is *Natalya, boyarskaya doch* (*Natalya, the Boyar's Daughter*).

Today's critics are inclined to believe that the events of this tale actually took place in a distant period of time—during the reign of Alexey Mikhaylovich (1645–76). The heroine, Natalya, is the daughter of kindly, honest Matvey, a Moscow boyar. One day in church she notices a handsome young man, Alexey. They fall in love, and Alexey asks Natalya to marry him, but in secret, since Boyar Matvey would refuse to give his consent, though Alexey does not explain why. Natalya's nurse helps them, so the lovers meet and elope at night. They are married in church and then ride to a forest, to a small lonely cottage which turns out to be Alexey's home. They are met by armed men, and the nurse thinks they have fallen into the clutches of robbers. At this point, however, Alexey tells Natalya his secret. His father, Boyar Lyuboslavsky, has been falsely accused of treason and threatened with a death sentence.

But an old friend helps the father and son escape. The boyar dies in a remote region, and Alexey decides to return to his homeland with the help of his father's old friend. There he settles down in his forest cottage. Alexey is sure that Natalya's father would not consent to his daughter's marrying the son of a disgraced boyar; however, he hopes to eventually prove the sincere loyalty of the Lyuboslavskys to the Tsar. His chance comes when Russia is attacked by the Lithuanians, and Alexey and Natalya (she is disguised as a man) go off to war. Alexey's daring and bravery inspire the Russian soldiers to defeat the Lithuanians. The Tsar wants to know the name of the courageous hero. It turns out that the Tsar already knows the formerly accused Boyar Lyuboslavsky to be innocent and is now anxious to reward his son. A touching scene ensues when Natalya meets her father, Boyar Matvey, who forgives Alexey and gives the couple his blessing.

Natalya, the Boyar's Daughter is one of the first Russian historical tales. Karamzin endeavors to reproduce the way of life and moral views of old Russia with incidents based on facts preserved in Russian legends dating back to the seventeenth century. According to literary scholars, Boyar Matvey is a real historical figure—Boyar A. S. Matveev—and Karamzin's tale is based upon the romantic marriage of Tsar Alexey Mikhaylovich and Natalya Kirillovna Naryshkina, Matveev's ward.[24] Of course, the historical treatment of the tale is nothing more than a free rendering of an actual episode from the past. What is important is that Karamzin sought his theme in Russian history and made an attempt to understand the special facets of the Russian national character. The writer is interested in the times when "Russians were Russians, when they wore their national costumes, even had their own way of walking, followed their own customs, spoke their own language, and spoke from the heart, that is, they said what they thought" (*SW*, I, 622). The same tenor of thought is retained in the story of the war with the Lithuanians and in the patriotic-heroic theme it introduces, which Karamzin weaves quite naturally into the fabric of his tale.[25]

It might seem that Karamzin idealized ancient Russia in that everything about the olden times looks so attractive and beautiful. However, a certain light irony was always present in his narration. The story itself about Natalya—by the author's own admission—"was what I heard in the realm of shadows, in the kingdom of the imagination, from my grandfather's grandmother."

Karamzin saw a kind of exotica in the old legends of the past, but at the same time he insisted that his tale was not something he dreamed up, but a story of actual events. In the conclusion, Karamzin relates that, while walking along the banks of the Moscow River, he found the tombstone marking the grave of Alexey Lyuboslavsky and his wife. Similar endings are later encountered in many other tales that are Sentimental in character.

The love story of Alexey and Natalya, and Boyar Matvey's relations with his daughter and with other people are depicted in sentimental and idyllic terms. All three characters possess only good qualities. All conflicts and obstacles barring the lovers' path to happiness are caused only by outer circumstances. From a psychological aspect, the most interesting moment is when Natalya must decide whether to run away secretly with Alexey and thus fail in her filial duty. This situation is typical of Classical literature: a struggle between duty and passion, in which a true hero would conquer his feelings for the sake of duty and win the right to the reader's regard and sympathy.

Because of the prevailing moral standards, Karamzin was prepared for the reader's reaction and condemnation of Natalya who had dared run away with Alexey and desert her "kind, sensitive, tender father." Karamzin even goes so far as to say: "Together with the reader we frankly blame Natalya, quite frankly reproach her. . . . But," he adds, "such love is fearful! It can turn the most virtuous person into a criminal! And whoever has been passionately in love, yet never in his life has done anything against virtue—he is fortunate! Fortunate, because his passion did not run counter to virtue; otherwise his virtue would have known its weakness, and tears of useless repentance would have run like rivers. The annals of the human heart assure us that this is the sad truth" (*SW*, I, 640).

In this tale, as in others, the theme of fate to which Karamzin turned time and time again is important. The virtuous Natalya was capable of committing an offense against morality and would have been blamed for her father's death had he died following the terrible news of his daughter's elopement. The reader is presented with a picture of the possible consequences of Natalya's rashness.

Describing the arrival of Alexey and Natalya at the forest cottage, Karamzin continues this play on the imagination. The nurse's suspicions that they have fallen into the hands of robbers take on a fleeting shade of reality for the reader. The author himself indicates that the coming plot development may follow the tradition of the adventure novel:

Now I could have put a terrible picture before the reader—innocence seduced, love deceived, a lovely but unhappy girl at the mercy of barbarians, murderers, as the wife of a robber chief and witness of terrible and villainous deeds, who after a life of torment finally dies on the scaffold under the poleaxe of justice before the eyes of her unfortunate father; I could have made all this seem quite probable, natural, and a sensitive person would have shed tears of sorrow and grief—but in so doing I would have been diverging from the historical truth my narrative was based on. (*SW*, I, 644)

In this way the author emphasizes the principal difference between his historical tale and the adventure novel.

The plot development leads to a happy denouement. Natalya's deed results in no serious consequences: Boyar Matvey does not die, he forgives his daughter, and is happy that she has a husband as worthy as Alexey turns out to be. All real conflicts (Boyar Lyuboslavsky's dishonor) as well as imaginary ones (the death of Natalya's father) are resolved. However, the possible tragic outcome of Natalya's story, indicated by the author himself, leaves its imprint on the mind of the alert reader.

A certain folklore stylization can be noted in the tale. Karamzin often makes use of fixed epithets characteristic of Russian folk stories: *krasnaya devitsa* ("fair maiden"), *dobry molodets* ("brave lad"), *ptichka rannyaya* ("early bird"), and so on. Karamzin's interest in folklore at the time was rather superficial; however, he saw in folk art the proof of that national originality which even then he resolved to champion in his own way. The peasants whom Natalya sees from her chamber window, in Karamzin's words, "have not changed at all up to this time: they dress the same, live and work just as they used to in the past, and with all the changes and donned guises they still show us the pure features of the Russian" (*SW*, I, 627).

In their folk art, the people preserve remnants of the distant past which Karamzin finds fascinating. However, folk art seemed rather primitive to him, and folklore could not fully satisfy him esthetically. He believed that folk compositions, old legends, and fairy tales were good only when skillfully retold and embellished to suit the taste of the educated connoisseur. Therefore, folkloric elements add only a certain coloring to his tale, whose style is a rather typical example of Russian Sentimentalism.

Both the author himself and his characters speak the "language of true sensitivity," their voices are "tender," they often sigh and shed tears. The tale reveals another essential feature of Sentimentalist style—irony, as already mentioned. With all his genuine sympathy for his heroes, Karamzin speaks of them at times with a tinge of humor. This is particularly noticeable when he describes the emotions of his heroine who is in love: "Natalya thought she had heard the young man sigh; at least, she had sighed," and "she did not eat at dinner, as is usual with people in love."

Karamzin uses a narrative style which resembles a running conversation with the reader. Sometimes remarks expected of the reader are introduced into the very text of the tale. For instance, the observation that Natalya went to church every day is followed by an unusual dialogue: " 'Every day?' the reader will ask. Why of course, that was the custom in the old days." The author tries to keep one jump ahead of the reader and explains in advance everything that might seem to him surprising or improbable. Natalya falls in love with Alexey at first sight, and the reader exclaims in disbelief: " 'In one minute! On seeing him for the first time, not exchanging a word with him?' " The author regards all this as quite possible, adducing the "force of mutual attraction." Karamzin advises anyone not convinced by this argument not to read the rest of the story: "Away, leave us, and do not read our story; it is meant only for those sensitive souls blessed with such sweet faith!" (*SW*, I, 634). It is significant that the author uses here "us," "our story," instead of "me" or "my," intentionally uniting himself with the sympathetic reader. He speaks for himself and his reader also when he declares: "*We* must believe Socrates," "*our* beautiful Natalya," "the reader and I frankly blame Natalya," and so on. In this way the reader becomes an active partner in the narrative and, thanks to this, the style of the tale acquires a certain liveliness and spontaneity.

This feature in Karamzin's narrative style was borrowed by subsequent authors; it took on special brilliancy in the works of Alexander Pushkin, who quite openly used some themes and motifs from *Natalya, the Boyar's Daughter*; and certain analogies, however superficial, can be made between Karamzin's heroine and Tatiana Larina in Pushkin's *Eugene Onegin*.[26] There were other elements in Karamzin's tales far more important for the subsequent development of Russian literature: an improvement in fictional prose style, the first attempts at psychological analysis, and the introduction of lyrical elements into the narrative.

The image of a fictional author, or narrator, always plays an important role in Karamzin's tales. A "sensitive person," he is nevertheless quite capable of taking a detached view of his emotions, sometimes treating them with irony. The author's cursory, at times humorous, remarks reveal his keenness of observation, his intellect, and his talent for introspection. Karamzin's feelings, thoughts, and moods while he was publishing the *Moscow Journal* either directly or indirectly shine through all the works he wrote at that time.

IV *Poetry and "Clever Thoughts" in Verse*

> Some images and topics from sheer necessity demand poetic form to give the reader greater pleasure, and there is not any euphonic, colorful prose that will do instead.
>
> —N. M. Karamzin

Prevalent among many readers and even literary historians of the nineteenth century was the widespread opinion that Karamzin's verses were merely "clever thoughts" put into verse that had almost no value as poetry. While Karamzin was given credit for introducing reforms into Russian prose, Ivan I. Dmitriev was considered the reformer of Russian poetry. However, far from everybody shared this point of view. Stepan P. Zhikharev, famous for his memoirs, wrote in 1807: ". . . Gavriila Romanovich [Derzhavin] alone admires Karamzin, defending him with might and main; others are either reticent about him or else say that he writes good prose; whereas our Karamzin also deserves respect for his poetry whose language is superb and full of feeling."[27]

In the history of Russian poetry, Karamzin's verse occupies a rather modest place but is nevertheless interesting in many respects. First of all, the autobiographical nature of Karamzin's lyrics was an innovation at the time. The poet's verses reflected thoughts and feelings directly related to events in his private life. In Russian poetry of the eighteenth century—even in love lyrics, not to mention the exalted genre of the ode—the prevailing themes were of a general and abstract character. As a rule, very little could be learned of the poet's private life from his verse. However, Karamzin's poems are rather like a lyrical diary, possibly the first of its kind in Russian poetry.

This may be noted even in his early verses included in his letters to I. I. Dmitriev. In March 1788, Karamzin wrote his friend about the coming of spring: "Soon everything will be alive again. Soon the birds, in choirs, will sing a paean to spring. Dear friend! How can we possibly be despondent? How can we possibly refrain from joining in the general rejoicing and say, with knitted brow."

> All round, all round us, sights of gladness,
> All round but merrymaking fest;
> While we, so burdened with our sadness,
> Through woodlands wander all depressed—
> We find no solace in the meadows,
> Gaze in a stream, tears fall from eyes,
> Round tears that trouble limpid waters,
> The waters rippling with our sighs.[28]

In a poem addressed to Petrov—*Anacreontic Poem to A. A. P.*, published in the *Readings for Children* in 1789—Karamzin appeals to a little breeze, half-humorously asking it to fly to his friend in the village and take him a message. The message refers to his pursuits and attempts to find his true calling: he first takes a stab at science and discovers he is not endowed with "Newton's talent"; then he turns to philosophy but with no success; and it is the same with his poetry:

> I thought to be a Thomson
> And sing the golden summer;
> But, ah! a quick confession
> I had to make, the essence:
> My voice had no quintessence
> Of Thomson's sweet expression.
> My singing was unbearable—
> Perforce, I sigh in silence.   (*CPW*, p. 69)

The poetry of Karamzin printed in the *Moscow Journal* is a deeper exposé of the moods arising from actual events in his personal life. In April 1791, influenced by a recent illness, Karamzin wrote his lines *To the Goddess of Health*. The poem *On Parting with P.* came to be written after Petrov's departure for St. Petersburg in 1791. The closing lines of the poem, addressed to his intimate friend, are in fact a lyrical monologue expressing the author's life credo:

> Farewell! Your friend you'll merit ere he die;
> Obeying truth, his soul at peace will lie:
> And none will ever say high rank he sought,
> Or with sweet words from titled scoundrels favors bought.
> To God alone he stoops to bend the knee;
> Fear of himself his only dole;
> Just worthiness claims his heart as true devotee,
> And you he loves with all his soul. (*CPW*, p. 105)

This strong urge for personal independence, for the preservation of self-respect, was not a pose, not the poetic formula of a romantically inclined young man. It rings with a sincere inner conviction which never left Karamzin throughout his whole life.

The death theme comes into this poem, which he wrote at the age of twenty-five: "Your friend you'll merit *ere he die*." It was not because the young poet wanted to set down his attitude to life once and for all, but because Karamzin was deeply involved in thoughts of death at the time. The poem was written on parting from his friend who was then gravely ill. It was not so much Petrov's leaving him as the premonition that they were parting forever which troubled and saddened Karamzin. This motif of alarm and grief stands out even in the opening lines of the poem:

> Struck the hour of parting, bitter chime!
> Farewell, my friend! One last, more time
> I press you closely to my heart;
> In silence weep one last, more time,
> Weep tears that Somber Fate has willed we part.[29]

The theme of fate, which plays a basic role in Karamzin's tales, also appears in this poem which is highly personal, even autobiographical, in character. Later, after Petrov's death, Karamzin revised the text slightly. The first three lines are unchanged, but then follows:

> I want to say: "Don't cry!"—and from my eyes tears start.
> But so Fate willed it to ensue;
> Farewell, may the Angel of Peace
> In the sigh of the zephyr
> Hover above you! (*CPW*, p. 104)

The words "Somber Fate" are changed for a more neutral tone: "so Fate willed it." The inescapable parting, the fear of losing his friend forever—these are retained; but the tragic tone is considerably softened by implying that "the Angel of Peace" brings quiet rest and assured trust in Divine Providence.

Though Karamzin's lyrics were mostly personal and intimate, he did not completely repudiate the social or civic motifs typical of Russian Classical poetry, as for example, his poem, *To Mercy*. This was a bold social act, for it was written in 1792, the year repressions were raging against Novikov and other Masons to whom Karamzin was bound by sincere friendship, although he had long since withdrawn from the activities of their circle. Appraising all the boldness of the poem, the well-known literary critic N. S. Tikhonravov wrote: "How much civic courage was needed at a time when the Novikov case had just begun to publish a poem in which a plea for enlightenment was so inseparably joined to a plea for freedom of thought and science!"[30]

The original text of the poem differed from the version printed in the *Moscow Journal*. Petrov wrote to Karamzin in July, 1792: "Please send me the poem *To Mercy* as it was originally written. I will not show it to anybody, if that is the requirement."[31] These lines testify that the original wording was even bolder in its political implication, and Karamzin had had to change some words for others less offensive.

To Mercy is a poem that reveals the author's political platform, and it differs essentially from the usual civic-patriotic odes. Lyrical rapture or exalted pathos is much mitigated, and the monarch is not portrayed as a creature standing on inaccessible heights. The poet addresses Catherine II as a creature of Earth, as a "tender mother" whose mercifulness can evoke "heartfelt tears." The poet is one of her subjects, but he is a human being like herself and, therefore, has the right to warn her against possible errors. The whole tone of the poem is keyed to this idea. It contains comparatively few Slavonic words; the rhetorical construction is correct and clear-cut; there are no digressions or superfluous episodes. The poem is not very long compared with the Classical ode. It begins with these lines:

> What holier than thou be given
> To mortals, what more lovely, sweet,

> Than thou, O Mercy, daughter of Heaven?
> Who could their heartfelt tears secrete,
> Or joyless, feel no admiration
> No stir of blood to sweet elation
> On gazing at your loveliness?   (*CPW*, p. 110)

Karamzin creates a certain mood that the reader must understand, not by applying logic, but by feeling all the allure of "Mercy" as a personification. The poet goes on to list the criteria which, he considers, Catherine the Great must meet as a truly just ruler, after which he promises glory and general gratitude:

> Whilst you to all give freedom holy,
> Nor dull the light of human minds,
> And that you trust the people wholly
> In all your actions is defined—
> The whilst be yours their adoration,
> Be glorified through generations,
> By all your faithful worshippers.

To express his lofty civic concepts, Karamzin tries to find a new medium without resorting to the ready-made poetic formulae of the Classical ode. The author speaks mainly about his own attitude toward the events he describes, appealing to the reader's emotions; thus, the social-political theme of the poem is also one facet of the poet's personal feeling.

The new principles embodied in Karamzin's lyrics were linked chiefly with the Sentimentalist trend, but pre-Romantic tendencies were also echoed in his poetry. For instance, Ludwig Kosegarten's poem *Des Grabes Furchtbarkeit und Lieblichkeit* so drew his attention that he wrote a free translation of it which he published in the *Moscow Journal* under the title *Mogila* (*The Grave*), retitled later *Kladbishche* (*The Graveyard*). Karamzin's poem was built around sharp contrasts. Gloomy pictures filling one with "horror and trembling" are counterbalanced with those describing "an abode of eternal peace" where tranquil serenity reigns:

> *First Voice:*
>
> Dark the grave, fearful; cold and distressful;
> Strong the winds' wailing; coffins are quaking;
> Rattle the bones bare and white.

Second Voice:
Still the grave, tranquil; quietly restful;
Soft the winds' breathing; no slumbers breaking;
    Grass grows and flowers delight.   (*CPW*, p. 114)

The second voice constantly refutes what the first has said. The concluding words belong to the second; and probably this is not accidental. The Sentimental poet identifies himself more with the soothing mood created by the final lines of a stanza. This is clear from the fact that the somber images, more typical of pre-Romantic poetry, seem to melt into the background, or at least are softened.

Karamzin found European pre-Romantic literature fascinating. His attraction to the *Songs of Ossian* is typical.[32] The Russian poet sought a personal interpretation of all he found in the songs of the Irish bard—dismal landscape, melancholy mood, pathos of emotions. Motifs from Ossian ring through Karamzin's poem *Raïsa*.

Raïsa is one of the first Russian ballads written. Its romantic story closely resembles Karamzin's *Poor Liza*; however, it receives different treatment because of the genre employed. The ballad opens with a vividly portrayed thunderstorm:

The storm went raging through night darkness,
Chain lightning flared through heaven's hood,
In black clouds thunder cracked with sharpness,
The hard rain clamored in the wood.

Then Raïsa appears, her face marked with despair. Climbing the escarpment overlooking the sea, she addresses a soliloquy to "dear, cruel-hearted Kronid." Raïsa recalls giving up her mother and father for his sake and the happiness his love brought her. But Kronid proved unfaithful and deserted Raïsa for Lyudmila. Raïsa is now searching for Kronid, calling to him in vain. Finally, in utter despair, she hurls herself into the sea.

The reader is told nothing definite about the characters in the ballad, unlike *Poor Liza* which describes the social background of both Liza and Erast and tells something of their way of life. There is no psychological motivation for Kronid's conduct and, for that very reason, his betrayal of Raïsa recalls Erast's unfaithfulness. The entire blame is put on the inevitability of fate: "But fate ordained it: for another/ You exchanged your Raïsa true" (*CPW*, p. 103). An indication of punishment for the one who causes another to suffer, as in Karamzin's tale, comes at the end of the ballad:

> . . . . Raïsa
> Plunged down into the sea. The thunder clapped:
> So Heav'n proclaimed the ruin
> Of him who wrought her ruin and death.   (*CPW*, p. 104)

Thus, all the main ideas of the tale are concentrated in a fairly short ballad, but the more compact rendering of the story and the use of the poetic genre combine to make the ballad the more dynamic of the two. Much of the ballad is devoted to landscape description. The lonely figure of Raïsa on the cliff overhanging the stormy sea, the lightning zigzagging through black clouds, create a picture which would—so the poet felt—make a strong impression on the reader's imagination. The sharp color contrasts catch the attention:

> And from her whitely gleaming breast,
> That trees had pierced with branches sharp,
> The hot blood streamed in rivulets
> Upon the green and humid earth.   (*CPW*, p. 102)

Raïsa's pale face, the "dead white" of her lips, contrasting with the "black clouds" and the flashing "chain lightning," are all hard colors without the tint or shade or transition-blending characteristic of Romantic paintings. These colors serve the intention of the poet who tries to portray a strong passion darkened by tragedy.

In the ballad, as distinct from the tale, the image of a narrator is absent, but the author's attitude to the events described is absolutely clear. His sympathy for Raïsa is evident from the epithets he selects: "poor Raïsa" and "her piteous moan." However, the heroine's agitated, passionate speech is in a language hardly typical of Karamzin, the lyrical poet.

For comparison, it is enough to turn to another of his poems written at this particular time—*Farewell*. Here the theme of betrayed love is given quite different treatment. The hero is passionately in love but, lacking social charm, fails to win the heart of his beloved. She marries another, and all the hero's hopes collapse. The poem ends with these lines:

In forests dense and dismal,
My whole life I shall dwell;
Cry out my grief abysmal,
And long for death—farewell!   (*CPW*, p. 113)

The conflict here lacks sharpness of outline and the tragic tension which seethes through the ballad *Raïsa*. The hero is far from experiencing the despair which drove Raïsa to suicide; and his intention to retreat into "forests dense and dismal" and cry out his "grief abysmal" (weep "streams of tears," if literally translated) is, in fact, more typical of the softer nature belonging to the "sensitive" man's personality. Also, the poem is tinged with a somewhat jesting, even ironical tone. For instance, the unlucky hero gets into a very amusing mix-up when he fails to realize that his emotion—love—is not taken seriously. The metrics (iambic trimeter with alternating masculine and feminine rhymes) give the poem a certain lightness and even gaiety.

In these poems, Karamzin working out one and the same plot conflict differently, puts each interpretation into a distinct form of style and imagery. He tries to find poetical forms that reflect all the varying human emotions and moods. Appropriate poetic form is particularly noticeable in his love lyrics, both in the verses mentioned which appeared in the *Moscow Journal*, as well as in later poems.

Karamzin's serious attachment for Princess Praskovya Gagarina inspired him to write his lyrical poems: *K vernoy* (*To the Faithful One*—1796) and *K nevernoy* (*To the Unfaithful One*—1796). At this time he also wrote his humorous verses *K samomu sebe* (*To Myself*—1795) and *Otstavka* (*Retirement*—1796), as well as his love songs, numerous impromptu fragments, madrigals, and inscriptions.

For a better understanding of Karamzin's esthetic views, one should study his poem *Protey, ili nesoglasiya stikhotvortsa* (*Proteus, or Inconsistencies of a Poet*). It is about the inevitable contradictions found in a poet's creative work:

But is not change the sensitive soul's one inborn asset?
The soul is soft as wax, as clear as looking glass,
Within it one can see all hues of Nature pass—
For you it cannot seem a solid mono-facet
Midst all the wonders Nature shows the world! (*CPW*, pp. 242–43)

Continuing, Karamzin graphically illustrates how diverse a poet's thoughts and feelings may be at various moments in his life and under different circumstances: now he admires the innocence of people of the "Golden Age," now the advances of the Enlightenment, then he sings of glory or is enraptured by the joys of love, and then he laments over treachery. Every theme is introduced as a perfectly independent fragment of the poem, and Karamzin changes the style and tone to conform to the theme. Here one can single out an idyll, there—a philosophic meditation or a love poem in elegiac meter. The principle which Karamzin used earlier, that of dividing a poem into "two voices" (*The Graveyard*), takes on greater complexity, no longer dual, but polyphonic. However, the author loses spontaneity and achieves only monotonous imitation—something like acting out an overly familiar role.

Incidentally, in *Proteus or Inconsistencies of a Poet*, Karamzin discloses certain of his writing techniques to the reader. Specifically, he admits that the original source of a poet's impressions and moods is "nature"—meaning the constant shifting of reality itself. This poem serves as a key to understanding all of Karamzin's poems.

In search of new forms which could convey the emotional diversity of poetical themes, Karamzin turns to meters which were either rarely used before or were completely new in Russian poetry. One can also notice a gradual evolution in Karamzin's poetry, an evolution linked with his original partiality for German and English poetry and later for French.[33] The use of the dactyl and blank verse was a typical feature of Karamzin's early poetry, guided as he was by the experiments of German authors (Goethe, Klopstock), and his early verses were mostly various combinations of the dactyl and the trochee. The poet was constantly experimenting in an attempt to overcome the monotony of the rhymed iamb. In one of his letters to Dmitriev, he even questioned the use of the Russian hexameter. "If you yourself," Karamzin wrote his friend, who was about to take part in a military campaign, "should ever think of glorifying your own great deeds and those of our whole army, then use the dactyl and trochee, or the Greek hexameter, but not iambic hexameter verses which are out of place in heroic poems and very tiresome. Be our Homer, but not our Voltaire. Two dactyls and a trochee, two dactyls and a trochee. For example:

Trúbÿ v pokhódë grëméli, kríki pó vózdükhü míchálís'
Trumpëts öf báttlë wëre shrílliñg, sh'outs through the aír mádly
                                                      whírliñg."[34]

Of course, the example given by Karamzin was rather artificial:
Too perfect a pattern does not conform to the hexameter style,
which implies the free interchange of the dactyl with the trochee.[35]
However, Karamzin touched upon the subject only in passing, with
no intention of making a detailed theoretical elaboration about the
problems of Russian prosody.

His unfinished heroic legend, *Ilya Muromets* (1794), is unique in
stylized folklore, with a very interesting rhythmic structure. The
poet attempted to reproduce the rhythm of Russian folk songs. He
warned the reader that the poem's "measure" (i.e., meter) was
"absolutely Russian" (lines of three trochaic metrical feet with a
concluding dactyl). But in reality, Karamzin lacked a sufficiently
clear idea of the peculiar rhythm of Russian folk songs. His fairy
tale or legend—both in sound and content—has very little in
common with authentic Russian folk compositions.

As time went on, Karamzin wrote fewer and fewer poems. They
became more traditional—mostly iambic and rhymed—reflecting
Karamzin's great interest in French poetry. To the end of his days,
the writer preserved an interest in poetry, but other facets in "versatile reality" attracted his attention even more. Events prompted
Karamzin to new ventures and new forms of literary activity.

CHAPTER 3

Letters of a Russian Traveller

I *The Literary Genre—"Travel Books"*

> Read Tavernier, Paul Lucas, Scharden, and other
> famous travellers who have spent nearly all their
> lives travelling: Do you find they have tender,
> sensitive hearts? Do they move your soul?
> —N. M. Karamzin

THE January 1791 issue of the *Moscow Journal* carried the first
extract from Karamzin's *Letters of a Russian Traveller*, and the
following issues continued to serialize them. The work proved to
be so long that when the *Moscow Journal* stopped publication in
December 1792, the end of the *Letters* had not yet been printed.
In 1794–95 a continuation appeared in the almanac *Aglaya* and,
finally, from 1797 to 1801 the *Letters of a Russian Traveller* came out
in a separate edition of six volumes.

The book was dedicated to the Pleshcheev family with whom
Karamzin had been friendly from the time of his intimacy with
the Masons. The work consists of letters written by the traveller to
his friends the Pleshcheevs. However, as literary researchers have
pointed out, the *Letters* are not representative of epistolary writing,
but are a rather carefully arranged series of travel notes and observations which Karamzin made during his tour.[1]

The odd combination of genres in the *Letters* necessitates a
background explanation. Diary entries were rewritten in epistolary
form, and correspondence often became a special artistic genre. It is
sufficient to recall the letters of A. M. Kutuzov and other Masons,
and Petrov's letters to Karamzin—letters that discussed, among
other things, philosophical, esthetic, and literary problems. For
Sentimental writers it was the most appropriate form, because
epistolary fiction (*The New Heloïse* by Rousseau, *Werther* by
Goethe) had reached its peak as a genre in epistolary verse.

To give unity to a large number of letters on differing themes called
for a definite design. A love story had determined the main contents

of letters comprising a novel, but a different design was given to the epistolary genre of travel books. The latter allowed the author the utmost freedom: he could easily pass from one description to another without bothering to preserve a sequence of events or unity of style. Sterne's *Sentimental Journey* (1768) became a classic example. A capricious play of the imagination, the shifting feelings and moods of the author actually became its main component, while the real journey itself receded into the background and was important only insofar as it provided those impressions that enriched the inner world of the narrator.

Sterne's name is often encountered on the pages of Karamzin's *Moscow Journal*, and when he published his translation of an extract from *Tristram Shandy*, Karamzin added a brief epilogue—a real panegyric to the English author: "Sterne, the incomparable! At what university of wisdom did you learn to feel with such subtlety? What rhetoric revealed to you the secret of moving the most delicate fibers of our hearts with a few words? What musician has such adept command over the sounds of strings as you have over our feelings?" (*SW*, II, 117).

Without doubt his admiration of Sterne had an important effect on Karamzin's creative work, above all on the *Letters of a Russian Traveller*. In the minds of many of his contemporaries, as well as his later readers, Karamzin was the "Russian Sterne." However, the resemblance between the two authors is not as close as it might seem at first sight.

The literary critic Vasily V. Sipovsky, who devoted an entire book to the *Letters of a Russian Traveller*, made a detailed study of European literary works which served as Karamzin's sources of inspiration in order to determine how much use he made of them. A wealth of factual information about the sights in European countries was picked up by the Russian traveller from various guidebooks, as well as from authors who had published a description of their travels through the same places—authors who, unlike Sterne, strove to give the reader some idea of what they had managed to learn of a country's history and what they saw there: cities, museums, parks, and so on. Sipovsky, however, came to the conclusion that "Karamzin [was] free of any taint of plagiarism. If he made wide use of guidebooks and other works, then in the eyes of Karamzin and his contemporaries this was more of a merit to his labor than a drawback."[2]

Karamzin wanted to give Russians a picture of European

countries, and this largely determined the character of the *Letters* which sets them noticeably apart from Sterne's *Sentimental Journey*. Besides, Karamzin laid no claims to writing a historical or geographical description of what he had seen—indeed, he stressed that he had no desire to do so—that for him something else was more important. In concluding his work, he wrote: "I am now rereading some of my letters: they are the mirror of my soul for all of eighteen months! After twenty years (should I live so long) it will be a pleasant mirror for me to look into—if only for me alone! I shall look and see what I used to be like, what I used to think and dream about; and what is more fascinating to a man (between you and me, let's admit it) than his own self? . . ." (*SW*, I, 601). This statement is interesting as a kind of personal declaration: a work must be "the mirror of the soul" and must reflect the author's individuality; outer facts and events are important only when they are connected with the writer's inner life. This declaration indicates why Karamzin called his work not merely "A Journey" but *Letters of a Russian Traveller*, which in itself implies a certain subjective approach to the narration. Thus, it is not a true "travel diary" genre, because Karamzin combines fact with fiction, a real journey with a journey of the imagination.[3]

Diaries and various travel notes were not new in Russia. Many Russians who had travelled abroad left notes of their impressions in memoirs, diaries, and letters. Among Karamzin's numerous predecessors was D. I. Fonvizin, whose *Letters from France* dating from the 1770's present a picture of political, economic, and cultural life in France drawn by a wise and alert observer.[4] The publicist prevails in Fonvizin's *Letters*, as he tries first and foremost to give an objective description and a sober appraisal of what he had seen. In this he differs from Karamzin, for whom the lyrical and emotional moment was more important than anything else. While Fonvizin's *Letters* come close to the genre of essays, one can never say this of Karamzin's *Letters*. The personality of the author himself is the focal point of Karamzin's work. Real incidents that happen to him while travelling provide material for constant meditations on the most diverse themes. It is difficult to single out which one is dominant, since the distinctive feature of Karamzin's *Letters* is its multifarious design. The shifting of scenes is linked with new impressions the author experiences, and this is sufficient inducement for shifting from one theme to another.

In addition, the narrative fabric is often interwoven with stories that could exist quite independently: they have their own plot, their own characters, and preserve a distinct unity of theme and style. Such, for example, is the novelette about Faldoni and Thérèse, the lovers from Lyons. In Karamzin's words the event took place "twenty years ago," that is, twenty years before he visited Lyons in 1790. Faldoni, a young Italian passionately in love with Thérèse, injures his jugular vein accidentally shortly before their intended marriage and, afraid that Faldoni might suddenly die, Thérèse's father refuses his consent to the marriage. The lovers decide on a suicide pact. Not far from Lyons near a village church, Faldoni meets Thérèse who has donned her wedding dress; here they shoot themselves simultaneously, using pistols entwined with crimson ribbons. Having told this story, Karamzin reflects upon the behavior ·of the lovers and confesses that "this incident terrifies rather than touches my heart" (*SW*, I, 358). The writer would have excused Faldoni's act if Thérèse had stopped loving him; he sums up as follows: "Faldoni and Thérèse! For me, you are an example only of frenzy, of insanity, of delusion, but not an example of true love!" (*SW*, I, 359).

Karamzin's attitude to the story of these lovers may be compared to the narrator's stand in various short tales, especially *Poor Liza*. There is a most direct relationship: Liza, who committed suicide, aroused the author's sympathy particularly because, unlike Faldoni and Thérèse, she had a good reason—Erast had married someone else.

The motif which preoccupied Karamzin (suicide over unhappy love) occurs again in another story introduced into the *Letters of a Russian Traveller*. At a certain home in Paris, the hostess told the writer about an unhappy girl, Alina, who was devoted to her lover, Milon, and took poison when he proved unfaithful. At the request of his hostess, the traveller puts the story into verse. And so the prose text of the *Letters* includes the poem *Alina*. This is not the only case; there are several poems in the *Letters* woven into the general fabric of the narrative.

Karamzin's style, which captivated his contemporaries in *Poor Liza* and *Natalya, the Boyar's Daughter*, was at its best in the *Letters of a Russian Traveller*. The diversity of topics brought out all the richness and versatility of his style. Some of the writer's contemporaries recognized the true value of the *Letters* as soon as the first chapters came out. For instance, Yakov B. Knyazhnin, a well-known playwright of the time, believed that "young Karamzin is creating a new, vivid, lively style, and is blazing a new trail in Russian literature";[5] and the prominent Moscow Mason Ivan V. Lopukhin, who undoubtedly knew about the differences that had arisen between Karamzin and other members of the Novikov circle, admitted in the preface to one of his books that he could have given a better account of his own thoughts and feelings "if he were endowed with the attractive, vivid, and splendid new style of the amiable Russian traveller."[6]

The *Letters of a Russian Traveller* preserve their coherence despite the varied and disparate elements of which they are composed, and this is proof of Karamzin's literary craftsmanship in creating a work of art interesting even today both to the Russian and the foreign reader.

II   *Europe Through Karamzin's Eyes*

> I travelled across Germany, sojourned and went on long walking trips in Switzerland, saw a good part of France, saw Paris, saw the free French people, and finally arrived in London.
> —N. M. Karamzin to I. I. Dmitriev

The first country with which the Russian traveller became acquainted was Germany. Knowing German well from childhood, Karamzin had long been interested in German literature and culture. He had prepared for the trip while still in Russia and knew beforehand where to go and what to see.

The writer visited the largest cities in Germany: Berlin, Dresden, Leipzig, Weimar, and Frankfurt am Main. Describing places of interest in these cities, he made use of historical and statistical information, freely and very originally weaving them into the fabric of his narrative. For example, talking about the residents of Dresden, the writer cites the population figure—about 35,000 people—"not very many for such a vast town and the size of the houses." To this he immediately adds a personal observation: "True, you don't meet many people in the streets, and only a rare house is without a notice about rooms to rent" (*SW*, I, 144). Describing the Dresden Art Gallery, Karamzin lists in detail all the pictures he saw, together with basic information about the artists—Raphael, Veronese,

Rubens, and others. Immediately he recalls a conversation he had with a guard, who told him that some ten paintings had recently been stolen from the gallery, but later had been recovered.

Karamzin tries to connect everything he sees with his earlier impressions or recollections. Looking at the monument to Gellert in Leipzig, he remembers reading the fables of this writer-philosopher in his childhood years, remembers how he laughed or cried over them, and remembers being introduced in Schaden's boarding school to Gellert's lectures on morals ("Moralische Vorlesungen").

In Germany, Karamzin focused his attention on problems of science, education, and book selling. He visited the University of Leipzig, where he himself had once wanted to study, heard a lecture on esthetics, and looked over the libraries and bookshops. Karamzin's stay in Weimar was highlighted by his meeting the most outstanding writers of the time, Johann Gottfried von Herder and Christoph Martin Wieland. He described his acquaintance with them minutely; he also recalled seeing through a window the "majestic Greek countenance" of Goethe, whom he did not succeed in meeting. That the chapters from the *Letters* on Germany were very important for Russian readers of the time may be judged from what Dmitriev wrote about Karamzin: "In the *Letters of a Russian Traveller*, he has introduced our young people to German literature, giving them a taste for the works of modern German writers, and turning them to a diligent study of the German language which has fallen into utter neglect."[7]

Despite his attraction to Germany, Karamzin also pointed out things about the country that gave him an unpleasant shock: he talked of the rudeness of German soldiers and condemned the sharp attacks made on other authors by Berlin writers and critics.

From Germany, the traveller set out for Switzerland, about which he also had a preconceived opinion. For Karamzin, it was "a country of picturesque nature, a land of freedom and prosperity." He was enthusiastic about Switzerland's beauty, its laws, and the simple customs of its people. Further on, Karamzin expatiates in detail about republican rule in Switzerland, talking about the Basel Republic where "bakers, shoemakers, and tailors often play an important role" (*SW*, I, 212), and giving a thorough review of the judicial system in Zurich. He described all this with evident sympathy, calling the Swiss a fortunate people and pointing out that farmers in the country were jolly folk and their fields productive. He mentioned the piety and cleanliness of the people in Zurich, and the absence of luxury: "The wise Zurich legislators," wrote Karamzin, "realized that luxury is sometimes the death of freedom, good morals, and manners and tried to bar its entrance into the Republic" (*SW*, I, 239).

However, not everything in Switzerland pleased him: in the people of Basel, he noticed a "pomposity resembling moroseness." He found the inscriptions on houses in Swiss cities rather funny and foolish. Another feature that jarred him: children frequently ran up to him and begged, not from need, but to get easy money. Thus, Karamzin's attitude toward Switzerland was mixed: The principles of republican rule aroused his admiration, but when discussing Swiss customs, he assessed them soberly and even critically. He seemed to see two Switzerlands: an actual and an imaginary one.

The reading of Gessner's idylls had in many ways predetermined Karamzin's attitude toward this country and at times his writing even takes on an idyllic tone. After visiting some Alpine herdsmen, Karamzin recalls the "Golden Age"—the blissful time when "all people were herdsmen and brothers"—and declares: "I would gladly forego many of the comforts of life (which we owe to the enlightenment of our day) to go back to the primitive state of man" (*SW*, I, 262–63). However, we should not take this statement at face value, but see it rather as a reflection of Karamzin's basic view. He had, after all, long admired the high educational standards of the Germans, spoken enthusiastically of the achievements of the human mind, and tried to bring world art to the reader. The "Golden Age" was nothing more than a beautiful dream, and the traveller's desire to remain with the Alpine herdsmen was only a momentary impulse.

Naturally, landscape comes to the fore in his description of Switzerland, and Karamzin views much of it through the eyes of those writers who had eulogized the beauty of Swiss nature—Gessner, Haller, and Klopstock. The Russian traveller visited the site where a monument to Gessner would soon stand; he read idylls and poems in the places where Gessner wrote them; and taking a walk around Lake Zurich, he remembered that Klopstock had written the ode *Züricher See* there forty years before.

In Switzerland Karamzin did not meet as many famous people as he had in Germany. But he became personally acquainted with Lavater, from whom he had once wanted to learn the meaning of life. Karamzin gives a detailed account of his talks with Lavater

and with another philosopher living in Switzerland—Charles
Bonnet. His stay of several months in Geneva gave Karamzin the
opportunity to closely observe the Swiss way of life and mores. His
letters from Geneva indicate that he had lost his former enthusiasm
for republican rule; and in place of his exalted worship of "the
country of freedom," one can see Karamzin's intention of painting
the character of the Genevese "in the darkest of colors." However,
he limited himself to a condescending and ironical remark: "May
their republic be a beautiful toy on earth for many long years"
(*SW*, I, 329).

Such a contradictory attitude to the republican system in Switzerland is understandable because from Geneva Karamzin went to
France where he became eyewitness to the events of the French
Revolution (1789–91). The first series of *Letters* published in the
Moscow Journal (1791–92) ended with a description of his arrival
in Paris. The sequel was published only two years later, which gave
the writer time to review the previously written material and
introduce several changes. Whereas his letters from Germany and
Switzerland were written more or less under the influence of direct
impressions, his letters from France and England told of events
separated by a considerable time gap.

It might seem surprising that Karamzin wrote comparatively
little about political events, especially since he visited France in
1790. Naturally, there were reasons. It must not be forgotten that
the French Revolution had seriously alarmed Catherine the Great
and most of the Russian gentry, who were still afraid of an insurgency
similar to the Pugachyov peasant revolt. Also, Karamzin was not
free to write about everything he had seen in France because of
censorship: fear of the "French infection" was so great that any
careless remark might have aroused the suspicion that it was
seditious.

All the same, one can learn many interesting and important
details from the *Letters* about the events in France. For example,
in Lyons, after attending a performance of Marie-Joseph Chénier's
Charles IX, where the king is portrayed as a weak and cruel man,
Karamzin remarks: "The author had in mind the latest developments, and every word concerning the present situation in France
was met with a storm of applause" (*SW*, I, 353).

Some years later, Karamzin wrote: "New republicans with
depraved hearts! Open Plutarch and you will hear from Cato, that

ancient, virtuous and greatest of republicans, that anarchy is worse than any kind of government!" (*SW*, I, 383). In these words Karamzin expresses his disappointment in the French Revolution, and only an echo remains of that enthusiasm with which he had regarded the revolutionary events at the beginning. Later he confessed to N. I. Turgenev that he had always been "a republican at heart"[8] and, naturally, was enthusiastic over the idea of establishing a republic.

When Karamzin was asked to write an article on Russian literature for the Hamburg journal *Le Spectateur du Nord*, he included extracts from *Letters of a Russian Traveller* not published in the Russian edition. The following statement is of special interest:

The French Revolution belongs to those events that determine the destiny of mankind for many centuries to come. A new epoch has been ushered in. I see this, and Rousseau foresaw it. Read one remark made in *Émile* and the book will drop from your hands. I hear splendid speeches for and against the revolution, but I am not going to imitate these bawlers. I must admit my views on this subject are not mature enough. One event follows another, like waves on a stormy sea, and people want to consider the revolution accomplished. No! No! We shall still see many startling events. The people's extreme agitation affirms it. I draw the curtain. (*SW*, II, 152–53).

Of course, much is left unsaid: to this day literary critics cannot with absolute certainty point out exactly which remark from Rousseau's novel *Émile* Karamzin had in mind. But at any rate there was no condemnation of the French Revolution in the writer's words, and his position undoubtedly "ran counter to the policy of government reactionary circles."[9] When Karamzin was in France in 1790, he managed to attend sessions of the Constituent Assembly despite obstacles that cropped up. He even attended "one of the most stormy sessions," sitting in his box seat for five or six hours (*SW*, I, 504). Apparently he had managed to see and hear Robespierre for whom he felt real awe, and reputedly, "on hearing the news of the death of the terrible tribune, he wept."[10] And yet, in his writing Karamzin spoke about "the horrors of the revolution," having watched the behavior of a raging mob, and with obvious sympathy told about seeing Louis XVI and the entire royal family in the royal chapel. The impressions of all he witnessed in revolutionary France aroused contradictory thoughts and feelings in the writer, and although he was a mere witness, he was hardly an impartial one. Saying good-bye to Paris, Karamzin admits: "Neither your Jacobins nor aristocrats did me any harm; I listened to arguments, yet did not argue myself; I visited your magnificent temples to please my eyes and ears" (*SW*, I, 507).

For all his interest in political problems, the Russian traveller paid no less attention to other facets of French life. He wanted to see cities remarkable for their history and architecture, visit places connected with the names of the most prominent French authors, become acquainted with the French theater, and observe the customs of the people. Karamzin gives an especially detailed picture of Paris, using various historical and literary sources. However, his task, as he saw it, was not to pass along all his knowledge of Paris to the fullest, but to tell the reader "how Paris looked to him in its present state." Everything drew his attention: luxurious Versailles, ancient churches, Rousseau's grave in Ermenonville and the ordinary, narrow, and dirty streets of Paris. But above all, Karamzin was interested in people—not the people "living in great mansions, but that majority living in garrets, in a cramped corner, in obscurity" (*SW*, I, 449). He tells about some of them, and in his "gallery of comment on deserving people" one can find a seller of playbills, a man who collected pins lost by ladies during theater performances, and a porter whose way of life and philosophy reminded him of Diogenes. Karamzin studied the behavior of the French people in the theater, talked with all kinds of people, visited one of the literary salons where a lady of fashion had her composition on love read. Many things amused the writer, and he was attracted by the inquisitive nature, wit, and gaiety of the French.

The description of England is markedly different from the preceding *Letter*s inasmuch as it lacks the feeling of freshness and spontaneity of perception which was still evident in his letters from France.[11] The form of the narration also changes accordingly, from notations of a diary character to occasional essays. Karamzin is, however, quite consistent in telling what places he visited in England, what he observed there, what people he met, and under what circumstances. As before, a good part is devoted to describing the sights: "In every city," he writes, "the most remarkable thing for me . . . is the city itself" (*SW*, I, 527). The traveller wrote a fascinating description of London and its environs: Howard Prison and the lunatic asylum are no less interesting to him than the Tower, Windsor Park, or Westminster Abbey. In his desire to give the reader a clear-cut picture of every side of English life, Karamzin divided his narration into chapters not connected with any particular date in his journey. They are short, separate essays: "The Stock Exchange and the Royal Society," "Parliamentary Elections," "Theater," "Family Life," "Literature," and so on.

Karamzin described the English political structure with obvious sympathy; and here, as in his positive comments on Swiss freedom, one can feel a veiled opposition to the Russian autocratic and bureaucratic system.[12]

Karamzin avoids stating definite opinions and tries to be impartial. For instance, while attending a parliamentary session, he concentrated on the behavior of the Members of Parliament and their manner of address. The writer recalled how much he had admired England in his youth. Now, on closer acquaintance, he regards England more critically and invariably singles out the one feature the English had that most appealed to him—enlightenment. The flourishing state of English commerce, the great variety of shops, and the cleanliness of London streets were things he noted, but the main factor, from his point of view, that spoke of the enlightenment of the English people was their family life. Karamzin admired the modesty of the women and the care that parents gave their children.

Prior to his trip to England, while he was still in Calais, he had searched for the room where Sterne had lived. It was shown to the Russian traveller by a young officer, and a peculiar dialogue ensued: " 'What would you like to see, sir?' a young officer in a parade uniform asked me. 'The room where Laurence Sterne once lived,' I answered. 'And where he ate French soup for the first time?' replied the officer. 'Chicken in sauce,' I answered. 'Where he praised the blood of the Bourbons?' 'Where his love of mankind brought a tender flush to his face?' 'Where the heaviest of metals seemed to him lighter than down?' "

Karamzin adds a comment to these lines: "All this is memorable to those who have at least once read Sterne's or Yorick's *Journey*; but can one possibly read it only once?" (*SW*, I, 510). And his trip to England began with his recollections of Sterne's *Sentimental Journey*, which he had read several times and knew almost by heart. The features of everyday life and conduct, and the carefully chosen historical and literary information all created quite an objective and skillfully etched picture of European life at the end of the eighteenth

century. This vast canvas depicts a great number of completely
different figures, and one must look at them closely in order to
appreciate the fact that Karamzin was a great master at literary
portraiture.

III   Portraits and Characters

> Fielding did not have to invent characters for his
> novels, but had only to observe and describe.
> —N. M. Karamzin

The tour gave Karamzin the opportunity of getting to know
different people—their lives, destinies, and characteristics. Outstanding philosophers and writers of the time, an innkeeper, a
maid, a fellow-traveller, a woman sitting beside him in a box at
the theater—every person met who was more or less remarkable for
something became one of the numerous characters in his Letters.
Karamzin's stories about famous people retain great historical
and literary value and at the same time are accurate and memorable
psychological studies. For example, he met Christoph Martin
Wieland, a German writer well known in Russia at that time.
Karamzin had been so delighted with Wieland's works that he called
his friend Petrov "Agathon" after the hero of Wieland's novel. [13]
No sooner had Karamzin arrived in Weimar than he hurried off
to see Wieland, and twice failed to find him at home. The following
day he went at eight o'clock in the morning and received a rather
cold welcome. Wieland admitted that he did not like to make new
acquaintances and even tried to ridicule the persistent young man
who wanted to discuss poetry with him. He told Karamzin that he
did not know how he should talk with him. "Perhaps," he added,
"you are my teacher in poetry" (SW, I, 176). Finally he relented and
asked Karamzin to come back. During his second visit, the Russian
traveller saw Wieland as a different man, friendly, kindly, and
sincere. Karamzin gives an exact account of the German writer's
opinions on literature and philosophy. He not only recalls what
Wieland said, but how he said it, and how he listened to his inter-
locutor. At the same time, Karamzin uses the parenthetic words
"seems," "seemed," as if to remind the reader that he was describing
the impression Wieland made on him, since it was not to be ruled
out that he had been mistaken or had incorrectly interpreted a

word or gesture. In addition, Karamzin gave the reader basic information on Wieland—his principal works, even unfavorable reviews, his success with the public, and Wieland's role in German literature.

The generally accepted opinion of Wieland as a major writer was just as essential to Karamzin as his personal impression on becoming acquainted with him. One complemented the other: the first giving maximum objectivity, the second stressing subjective perception.

During the trip, Karamzin met some Danes: the naturalist Gottfried Becker, the poet Hans Baggesen, and Count Adam Moltke. They were his travelling companions for some time, and each was characterized in the *Letters*.[14] Becker was a clever, interesting conversationalist who fell in love easily and spoke with humor about his amorous failures. Karamzin includes several amusing episodes about Becker's romantic exploits.

The other two Danes, Baggesen and Moltke, provoke a different reaction from the author of the *Letters*. With obvious irony, Karamzin describes their bizarre behavior and their affectations. For instance, during a walk in the environs of Geneva, Moltke, "looking at Mont Blanc, raised his hands and, expressing his rapture with loud exclamations, assured us he would like to live and die on its snowy crest; he was surprised that none of the earth's great rulers, to win undying glory, had ever thought of building a wide road from the foot to the top of the mountain so that people might drive there in carriages." Karamzin's ironic remark is: "You can see that the count is fond of gigantic ideas!" (*SW*, I, 323).

Karamzin did not always have the chance to get to know a person who interested him. During his travels he gradually developed the journalist's art by putting his questions cleverly, and from the answers, no matter how laconic, would build the story of somebody's life. Based on his encounters with real, living people, Karamzin created definite literary types. The character of an innocent, virtuous girl of "humble origin" always takes on idyllic features in the *Letters*, reminiscent of his *Poor Liza*.

Despite Karamzin's depiction of distinctive features of every country, he tries to find in every person he meets something common to all humanity, irrespective of social origin or nationality. The author's attitude to the characters he depicts in the *Letters* is determined not by a preconceived opinion but by their conduct, words, and actions. Although he quotes a stranger's words and gives objective facts, he does not relinquish his role as interpreter, and his subjective thoughts and feelings about various persons are of primary importance. It is natural, therefore, that the main hero of the *Letters* turns out to be the Russian traveller himself.

IV   *The Image of the Author*

> I shall look within . . . and see what I used to be, what I thought and dreamt. . . .
>
> —N. M. Karamzin

Since the *Letters* represent the personal diary of Karamzin, the image of the author is its focal point. Because work on the book extended over several years, it is difficult to construct the author's character from the *Letters*. The tour itself lasted a rather long time, and almost every day brought with it new acquaintances and new impressions which to a greater or lesser degree influenced the forming of young Karamzin's mind.

Working from his original notes at a much later time, Karamzin viewed many things through different eyes; more recent thoughts, feelings, and moods imperceptibly blended with the former conception of the canvas. In other words, a new image was superimposed upon the original, resulting in a rather complex contamination or fusing of the two: an image comprising features representing the author from the past and from the present.

The complexity of this image is also due to the fact that the author of the *Letters* did not always express the real ideas of Karamzin himself. As in his tales, the narrator is a man who resembles Karamzin in many ways, yet is not Karamzin. The play of imagination, typical of the writer in his earlier works, is also present in the *Letters*; with all his desire for utmost sincerity, Karamzin is often carried away and at times fictionalizes—writes less about what he is really like than about what he would like to be.

However conflicting—at first glance—certain ideas about civilization and other matters seem, on the whole Karamzin upholds his viewpoint rather consistently. His dream of the Golden Age, when people tasted all earthly joys to the full, remains but a dream. In reality, he affirms that the progress of civilization is connected with the growth of science, art, and culture. This is Karamzin's main point of view, and he is sure that enlightenment is always beneficial. His desire to meet outstanding scientists and writers, and to visit the places connected with their creative works speaks for itself.

Pondering over the possible degradation of France, "the most beautiful country in the world," the writer remarks: "One thing comforts me—the fact that with the decline and fall of nations, the whole race of mankind does not fall; one people yield their place to another, and if Europe should fall into desolation, then in the heart of Africa or in Canada new political societies will flourish, as well as the sciences, crafts, and the arts" (*SW*, I, 363). This preference of civilization to savagery, distinctly expressed here, was characteristic of Karamzin both in the period of publishing the *Moscow Journal* and later.

The *Letters of a Russian Traveller* often do expose Karamzin's real thoughts. He stands out as an advocate of enlightenment, for he believes that the spread of knowledge and development of science, literature, and art all serve to improve and perfect man. Speaking of the French Academy of Science and its leading representatives, Karamzin declared: "I am always ready to weep with heartfelt joy when I see how science unites people living in the north and south, when I see how they love and respect each other without knowing each other personally. No matter what misologists say— science is a holy affair!" (*SW*, I, 424).

While intellectual matters were always valued highly by Karamzin, he directed his attention to the sphere of emotions. Works of art and the destinies of the people he met were all of primary interest to him because they were able to "touch his heart."

Asceticism was alien to Karamzin. Relating the sad, secluded life of the recluse monks in a Carthusian monastery at Lyons, he remarks that "the founders of this order had a poor knowledge of man's moral nature, created, so to speak, for action without which we shall find neither serenity nor pleasure, nor happiness" (*SW*, I, 350). He remains a fixed enemy of any kind of fanaticism, superstition, or religious intolerance. Finding himself in a Benedictine monastery in Frankfurt, Karamzin gives free rein to his imagination, seeing fanaticism personified: "A monster in all its infamy, its hair standing on end from rage, foaming at the mouth, eyes crazed and flaming, with a dagger in hand aimed straight at its heart" (*SW*, I, 183).

Karamzin did not deny religion, nor could he agree with the atheistic views of Voltaire, though he considered it the great

merit of the French writer that he "propagated mutual tolerance of
faiths" and "disparaged infamous false beliefs" (*SW*, I, 289).
Animosity over differences in religion was just as unacceptable to
Karamzin as the aim of asserting the superiority of one nation over
others. He valued the accomplishments of civilization and culture
irrespective of the nation they belonged to; the important thing
was to make them available to all humanity. This inner conviction
of Karamzin was connected with his approach to his personal
travels—as if the author of the *Letters* were carrying out the mission
of an intermediary between Russian and European cultures.

This idea is expressed in the *Letters* in two ways: first, the traveller
tried to understand the peculiarities of every people and culture;
second, he held it very important that he was Russian. The thought
of his fatherland never left him: listening to songs on the banks of
the Rhône, he found them akin to Russian folk songs; looking at
the monument to Louis XIV, he recalled Peter the Great; in Paris,
he watched with great interest and attention the melodrama *Peter
the Great*, which "had very moving scenes, at least for a Russian"
(*SW*, I, 396); he told Leipzig scientists with great pride about the
Russian translation of Klopstock's poem *The Messiah*.

The *Letters* are to a certain extent imitative—a literary work in
epistolary form rather than a collection of real letters. Karamzin
tried to build an illusion that the letters he published were real
and not arranged diary notes. To support the illusion he uses a
simple method: he continually addresses his friends, muses over his
affection for them, and so on. The theme of the author's friends
becomes a unique ornamentation in the *Letters* as both a literary
device and an expression of the writer's sincere feelings.

In the very first letter the friendship theme becomes the central
focus. The author recalls how he said good-bye to "his dear friends"
the Pleshcheevs, how Petrov escorted him to the end of town, and
how he felt that he had "become an orphan in the world, an orphan
in his soul" (*SW*, I, 82). In his first letters, Karamzin tells his friends
how much he misses them, but several days later he confesses:
"I love you, my dear friends, as much as ever; but I find the separation not so saddening after all. I am beginning to enjoy my journey.
Sometimes I sigh when I think of you, but a light breeze slips over
the water in the same way without disturbing its transparency.
Such is the human heart; at this very moment I thank my stars
that it is like that" (*SW*, I, 105). This confession justifies the change

of mood that follows in his letters; often they bear no salutation at all, and the theme of friends appears only on occasion.

While taking his travel notes, Karamzin did not merely set down actual everyday events, but also the moods that swayed him under varying circumstances. And when he was preparing the text for publication, he skipped certain subjects and "added color" to others, to use his own words.

At times, he gives full rein to his imagination and tells the reader not what he really saw, but what he might have seen; and, consequently, not what he really felt, but what he might have felt. For instance, seeing an ancient castle of a robber he imagines a whole scene: The robber returns home with his loot, his wife and daughter meet him and rejoice at the stolen riches, and the unlucky travellers who fell victim to the robber are imprisoned. Suddenly the writer interrupts his flight of imagination and brings the reader back to earth: " 'Stop, imagination!' I said to myself and—paid two farthings to the dried-up old woman and ugly boy who were showing me round the castle. It has long been deserted and is beginning to fall into ruin" (*SW*, I, 115).

Reflections on what might have happened but did not, occupy the author even when he talks of himself, his feelings, and moods. The chapter on his visit to Windsor Park is interesting in this respect. Resting in the shade under some trees, the traveller dreams of the future—of love and fame, the "two idols of sensitive souls." Sadness intermingles with his thoughts, awareness of the impossibility of happiness, of the inevitable separation from one's beloved, of the grief that accompanies fame. Karamzin comes to the conclusion that "our life is divided into two periods: the first part we spend in the future, and the second in the past" (*SW*, I, 554). Obviously, Karamzin could not have set down all these reflections during the tour, but to retain the illusion, he concluded his meditations with the following words: "So my thoughts ran in Windsor Park, as I analyzed my feelings and speculated that all these would be mine, in time!" (*SW*, I, 555).

While seeing the sights, the traveller frequently liked to think about the past and picture scenes of the past in conjectured detail, as in the above example about the robber's castle. This was one of the devices Karamzin used to create a particular mood in himself. Literary association was another device the author used even more often. Finding himself in those places where authors whom he had read used to live or stay, Karamzin tried to immerse himself in the same feelings they experienced there. After visiting the monument to Gellert, the traveller wrote: ". . . I shall not go in to dine. I shall sit under the window and read Weisse's *Elegy on the Death of Gellert*, the odes by Kramer and Denis;[15] I shall read and give way to my feelings and perhaps—weep!" (*SW*, I, 160).

Describing nature, Karamzin often falls under the influence of his literary predecessors, looking at landscapes through their eyes. However, he repeats what others have said only if his own impression coincides with theirs. It is as if he were checking up on what he learned from books, using the criteria of personal experience. An example typical of this is his observation of a sunset in Switzerland. Having noticed that the mountain crests lit by the setting sun took on all colors of the rainbow, the writer remarks: "Now I understood Haller's verse: "Und ein Gott ist's, der Berge Spitzen röthet mit Blitzen!" (God paints the mountain crests with lightning —*SW*, I, 251). Karamzin put what he had observed in one of his own poems: ". . . Solnechnyi luch osveshchaet/ Gor nepristupnykh khrebet raznotsvetnyi." (". . . A bright ray of sunshine illumineth/ Remote rainbow-crests of the mountains.")

This example shows how a poetic image was born in Karamzin's mind. Haller's verse is no more than a starting point. The verse is recalled at the precise moment he is watching the phenomenon which attracted Haller's attention. Literary erudition does not interfere with Karamzin's observation and imagination, but helps him notice much that might otherwise have escaped his field of vision.

Some critics regarded the *Letters of a Russian Traveller* as being extremely subjective in character. However, even a cursory acquaintance with the *Letters* shows that their content was so extensive and serious that they could have served the Russian reader of the day as a kind of encyclopedia, introducing him to the history, political structure, art, and literature of the countries of Europe. All this was offered in the *Letters* through the prism of the author's vision. The reader continually saw before him a living person— wise, educated, gifted with a sense of humor, capable of tender affection, and able to see nature's beauty.

CHAPTER 4

Collected Works and Almanacs—
1794–1801

I *Continuing as a Publisher*

Dear readers, dear ladies and gentlemen, your
enjoyment, your appreciation is for me a precious
garland.

—N. M. Karamzin

T HE success of the *Moscow Journal* proved how interesting the
Russian public found the works of young Karamzin. The work
involved in publishing demanded great effort; the necessity of
preparing each issue of the journal by a press deadline was a burden
for the writer; thus, at the end of 1792 he closed down the
publication. Unfavorable conditions, specifically censorship, probably also contributed to the demise of the *Moscow Journal*. But the
end of the journal did not mean the end of his literary work; indeed,
Karamzin had wanted more free time for creative writing. In a
journal which included works by other authors, he could not
fully express his own individuality as a writer. He had written
enough to win a good reputation among the reading public; now
he felt that the time was ripe to publish his own book.

The idea of personally publishing a separate volume of one's
own works was not new in Russia. A number of authors had
published collections of their verses in the 1770's, mostly collections
of odes or verse divided strictly according to the traditional hierarchy of genres: first, sacred odes; then paeans of praise; and only
then epistles, elegies, idylls, and other genres. Accordingly, the title
usually was *Selections* or *Odes*, and frequently a book was dedicated
to a member of the royal family or to a patron of the arts from the
nobility.

The elegant edition which appeared in 1794 had very little in
common with such collections. The first of Karamzin's selected
works, it was a book in two parts of small format under a rather

strange title: *Moi bezdelki (My Trifles)*. The writer included a
number of pieces he had published earlier in the *Moscow Journal*,
but not nearly all of them. Consisting mostly of poetry and tales,
there could be no question of adhering to the hierarchy of genres,
since Karamzin's verses rarely met genre criteria. The title of the
collection itself was a kind of declaration through which the author
emphasized the unorthodox and intimate character of his book.[1]
The new approach was soon copied by many other Russian authors,
among them, I. I. Dmitriev who entitled his collection, published in
1795, *And My Trifles*.

Karamzin's book enjoyed no less success than the *Moscow
Journal*, for it became available to a much wider circle of readers
who had been unable to subscribe to the periodical. The impression Karamzin's first book made in the Russian provinces was
recorded by F. N. Glinka, a poet and cousin of Mikhail Glinka,
the famous composer:

> As much as I personally remember of my early childhood, people read
> very little in our quiet neighborhood near the town of Dukhovnitsy in the
> Province of Smolensk. And outside of religious books, there were no others.
> Suddenly, *My Trifles* came into our home. The book was sent to us from
> Moscow, and how can I describe the impression it made? Everybody
> simply pounced on the book and buried themselves in it: reading, reading,
> and rereading until finally we all knew it by heart. From our house, the book
> made the rounds of all the neighbors and came back to us with the pages
> falling out.[2]

While preparing this selection of his earlier works for publication,
Karamzin also worked on his almanac, and two issues of the almanac
Aglaya came out in 1794–95, containing almost exclusively new
works by him.

This period was also marked for Karamzin by sad events: His
friends, Novikov, Turgenev, and other Masons were being harshly
repressed by the government. In 1793, his closest friend, Petrov,
died. Serious financial difficulties which beset the Pleshcheevs and
the illness of Anastasia Ivanovna also grieved and distressed him.

These personal troubles increased Karamzin's confused state of
mind, shaken as he was by the turn of revolutionary events in
France. The ideas of Enlightenment underwent a sudden and
radical change in France, which Karamzin could not accept.

His world outlook underwent an important crisis: his dreams of freedom in the abstract seemed unsound, and his belief in a possible rational reconstruction of society was shaken.

His first and most immediate reaction was an attempt to withdraw into a shell of personal feelings and interests. In the almanac, Karamzin's desire to speak "the language of the heart" predominates even in the epigraphs and dedications. For example, the first almanac opened with an epigraph taken from Charles Bonnet: "Les esprits bien faits qui ne peuvent lire mon coeur, liront au moins mon livre."[3] The second was dedicated to "The friend of My Heart," Alexandra I. Pleshcheeva.

With the exception of three poems, the works printed in the almanacs were Karamzin's own original writings, not translations. Many were autobiographical in character, especially the prose sketch, *A Flower on the Coffin of my Agathon*, written in memory of Petrov. The writer recalls the years of his youth when he became Petrov's friend, their talks, cites an extract from a letter Petrov sent him, and tells of Petrov's death as related by someone who was present. It is a lyrical sketch including a large number of exact details which reveal the two men's affection for one another.

The remaining material published was also tied in with Karamzin's personal feelings and moods, for instance, the theme of Agathon connected with the essay *Athenian Life*, a poetic dream in which even the author himself does not believe. A direct reflection of contemporary political events can be found in the epistolary essays *Melodor to Philalet* and *Philalet to Melodor*, which are also personal, as noticed by Novikov when he wrote Karamzin that in Melodor he saw Karamzin himself and in Philalet, Petrov. To this Karamzin answered: "I often thought of the unforgettable Petrov . : . so it is not surprising that you found his portrait in my Philalet."[4]

The almanac fused individually plotted works of differing genres into a harmonious whole, since certain themes and motifs linked them together, and a general tone and mood suffused them. The meaning and sense of each work, taken separately, is materially enlarged if viewed in the context of Karamzin's other prose sketches, tales, and poems in the almanac.

In contrast to the collection *My Trifles*, *Aglaya* contained hitherto unpublished works. The writer succeeded in presenting a whole lyrical range, and the almanac became a book that helped the reader acquire a fair notion of the author's inner spirit.

Although he selected only original works for *Aglaya*, Karamzin did not neglect bringing the works of Western European authors to the Russian public. He issued in a separate edition the *New Tales* of Jean François Marmontel (Parts 1 and 2, 1794 to 1798) which he had previously translated and published in the *Moscow Journal*. In 1796, Karamzin's translation of Madame de Staël's story *Méline* appeared, dedicated to A.I. Pleshcheeva, as was the second book of *Aglaya*. Throughout 1795, the writer was an active contributor to the *Moscow Gazette*, which published his translations from foreign periodicals in its "Miscellaneous" section.

Meanwhile, Karamzin was preparing a Russian *Almanac of the Muses*—a first anthology of Russian poetry. Toward the close of 1795, he wrote Dmitriev about his plan: "Let us clear a stage for Russian poets where they can make a public appearance without shame."[5]

The writer had no predecessors in such an undertaking, but his publishing experience, literary and personal contacts with prominent authors, a fine esthetic taste, and a lively interest in poetry helped him in his new venture. The anthology came out under the title *The Aonides, or a Random Collection of New Poems* (Parts 1–3, 1796–99). Karamzin's collection did not include the well-known poets of the recent past, but all the most significant contemporary poets, including himself, were represented.

The publisher's preface to the second book of *The Aonides* was a unique manifesto of Sentimental poetry in which Karamzin spoke of two main shortcomings of contemporary poetry: The first was "superfluous pomposity, a thunder of words quite out of place." He had in mind, above all, works by those epigones of Classicism, the authors of bombastic odes. The second fault was "lachrymose affectation." As Karamzin explained: "There is no need to constantly talk of tears, selecting various epithets to describe them, calling them 'glistening' or 'like diamonds'—this is an unreliable method of arousing pity."[6]

This statement seems to run counter to the personal practice of the Sentimentalist writer in whose works tears and sighs played a rather important role. However, this declaration did not mean that Karamzin rejected his former literary principles. He was, however, criticizing the works of authors who tried to write under the banner of the new trend by using ready-made, trite formulas. Tears and sighs were only superficial signs of Sentimental poetry; beneath them

lay something much more profound. Karamzin was convinced that
the poet must "describe not merely the general attributes of grief,
[for they are] too commonplace to make an impact on the reader's
heart, but [must] find the special emotional expression that fits both
the character and the circumstances created by the poet."[7]

Aonides, Aglaya, and *My Trifles* were soon published in second
editions, and the *Letters of a Russian Traveller* came out in book
form (Parts 1–6, 1797–1801).

Karamzin did not have an easy time carrying out his publishing
and literary activities during this period. He had never enjoyed the
special favor of the Empress, and his connection with the Masons
aroused serious suspicion on the part of the government. In the
summer of 1795, when he was vacationing in the country, it was even
rumored that he had been exiled. However, Karamzin was never
involved in the investigation against members of Novikov's circle.
In 1796, Catherine the Great died and Paul I succeeded to the
throne, but the change did not make Karamzin's position much
better. Under Paul I censorship grew even more strict, and the
authorities saw too much "freedom of thought" in the works of the
writer even more frequently. At the close of 1798, Karamzin wrote
Dmitriev in despair: "Probably the censors would like to delete
or make changes in the new editions, but I would rather throw
everything over than agree to such an infamous transaction; if
things go on this way, in a year's time there probably won't be a
single one of my books on sale."[8] Yet, he soon completed two
new and important literary projects. In 1798, he translated and
published an anthology in three volumes, *The Pantheon of Foreign
Literature.* In 1801, the *Pantheon of Russian Authors* came out.
In compiling it, Karamzin had based his information on N. I.
Novikov's *A Trial Historical Dictionary of Russian Writers* (1772),
which was more of an encyclopedia, but in evaluating the works
of nearly every author, the *Pantheon* had brought the material up
to date.

The *Pantheon of Russian Authors* was the first attempt at dividing
Russian literature into periods. In his article on the satirist A. D.
Kantemir, Karamzin wrote: "Dividing our literary style into
epochs, the *first* must begin with Kantemir, the *second* with Lomonosov, the *third* with the Slavic-Russian translations of Mr. Elagin and
his numerous imitators, and the *fourth* with our times, when a
pleasing style [*priiatnost' sloga*] is developing" (*CW,* II, 162). Much

in this period division may seem strange and unconvincing to modern-day literary historians, i.e., devoting a separate "epoch" to a second-rate writer like I. P. Elagin. However, Karamzin's interest in his native literature and his desire to subject it to critical review was certainly of extreme importance to both Russian literature and Russian criticism. The guiding principle for Karamzin in setting up demarcation lines between the different epochs was the question of style—for him the decisive criterion. Contrasting his own epoch with all those preceding, Karamzin conceived his own literary work as a new stage.

II *Philosophic Reflections*

> But time and experience destroy the castles in the air of youthful years.
>
> —N. M. Karamzin

The thirst for knowledge and a desire to become thoroughly versed in all aspects of European culture, characteristic of the young Karamzin, stemmed from his conviction that science and art made people better and happier and brought them only good. He saw mankind's development as an untiring march forward and saw the eighteenth century, compared to the preceding ones, as the Age of Enlightenment and of triumphant progress. No serious doubts assailed him even during his travels through revolutionary France. However, the establishment of the Jacobin dictatorship in the spring of 1793, which threw many Russian intellectuals into confusion, forced Karamzin to give serious consideration to the problem of making social and political utopias realistic.[9] It was impossible for him to relinquish his former ideals; however, the theory demanded some adjustment or other, but could not be totally discarded, otherwise his activities would have become meaningless to him. Karamzin continued his creative work despite all the doubts and inner conflicts that tormented him at this time, and they became the theme of his new works.

The frankest expression of the writer's philosophic ideas are to be found in his articles in the almanac *Aglaya—Melodor to Philalet* and *Philalet to Melodor, Chto nuzhno avtoru? (What is Necessary to an Author?)* and *Nechto o naukakh, iskusstvakh i prosveshchenii (Something about the Sciences, Arts, and Enlightenment)*—and in his essay *Razgovor o schastii* (*Discourse on Happiness*) (1797), published separately.

Karamzin again turned to the epistolary genre, but used a different approach than the one in *Letters of a Russian Traveller*. Now it was not the lyrical diary of a single hero, but correspondence between contrasting characters, Melodor and Philalet, each expressing what seemed to be opposite viewpoints. However, as critics have already pointed out, "the voices of Karamzin's own soul" resound through the letters of both Melodor and Philalet.[10]

Melodor's letter tells about "ruined hopes and plans." It speaks of the important achievements of mankind during the eighteenth century: "the light of philosophy, moderation of manners, a refinement of intellect and feelings, an increase in the comforts of life, the general spread of a communal spirit, close and friendly national relations, a milder form of government, and so on and so forth" (*SW*, II, 246). All this promised the advent of "the kingdom of wisdom," but against expectations comes catastrophe. Melodor exclaims in despair: "Oh, Age of Enlightenment! I do not recognize you—in bloodshed and flames, I do not know you—among murder and destruction, I do not know you!... (*SW*, II, 247).

These words later found a strange echo in Radishchev's poem *Eighteenth Century:*

No, you will not be forgotten, Oh age of both wisdom and wildness,
You will forever be cursed, a surprise everlasting for all.
Blood in your cradle runs red; all your lullabies—thunder of battles.[11]

Radishchev took an entirely different stand when describing the eighteenth century, but the French Revolution left him deeply dissatisfied and disappointed. Despite all the fundamental differences in the attitudes of the two writers toward contemporary events, Radishchev used motifs and images resembling those Karamzin depicted so vividly in Melodor's letter.

More than half a century later the well-known Russian liberal writer Alexander I. Herzen, who lived many years in exile, cited Melodor's letter in the introduction to his book *From the Other Shore*, finding Karamzin's work in accord with his own thoughts and moods.[12] Herzen had experienced the same collapse of hopes after the failure of the French Revolution of 1848 and understood and felt close to the words of Karamzin's Melodor. "We thought

the close of our century would see the end of mankind's major
troubles, and believed it would bring about a joining of theory and
practice, of theorizing and action. . . . Where is this consoling philosophy now? It was demolished at its foundation; the eighteenth
century is drawing to a close, and the wretched philanthropist
measures out, with two steps, his grave to lie in, with a heart deceived
and torn apart, there to close his eyes forever" (*SW* II, 246–47).

Karamzin tried to overcome the agonizing doubts resounding
throughout Melodor's letter by countering this tragic world outlook with another point of view expressed by a different imaginary
correspondent—Philalet, who disproves many statements made
by Melodor. Philalet is also disappointed with his century and
admits that the minds of his contemporaries are subject to "horrible
delusions." However, he is convinced that "enlightenment is always
beneficial; enlightenment always leads to virtue . . . and serves as an
antidote for all the disasters of mankind" (*SW*, II, 256–57).

Earlier, Karamzin had no doubts whatsoever as to the benefits
of enlightenment. Now, at the moment of his reappraisal of spiritual
values, this question stood out in all its poignancy, stopped being
an axiom, and demanded proofs. It was necessary to substantiate
the thesis propounded in Philalet's letter with greater thoroughness.
More solid arguments had to be opposed to the theory of Rousseau
who denied that the sciences and arts promoted the betterment of
man in his discourse *Si le progrès des sciences et des arts a contribué
à corrompre ou à épurer les moeurs.*

Karamzin devoted a special article to polemics with Rousseau,
Something about the Sciences, Arts, and Enlightenment, directing
it not so much against Rousseau, whom he considered "a great
man," as against "ignoramuses who discredited enlightenment
under the aegis of this renowned citizen of Geneva" (*SW*, II, 123).
Yury M. Lotman, who did research on the Russian attitude to the
heritage of Rousseau, pointed out that the appearance of Karamzin's
polemic article in 1793 had its reasons: "He feared that the tactics
of the Revolution—and its acts of bloodshed—would be used to condemn the inevitable and, in Karamzin's opinion, salutary people's
movement which was advancing along the road of progress."[13]
Karamzin was trying to uphold the idea of progress against his
most dangerous enemy—himself. Karamzin's discourse on the
sciences and arts was an extensive, detailed, and well-reasoned
answer to the doubting Melodor. Thus, the essay complemented

Philalet's letter, because Philalet had not managed to give a sufficiently minute account of his views concerning Rousseau's theory.

Karamzin's article *What Is Necessary to the Author?* is closely linked to the above works. In it, Karamzin clarifies his attitude toward Rousseau. "Why do we like Jean-Jacques Rousseau, with all his weaknesses and delusions? Why do we like to read him even when he is dreaming or is tangled up in contradictions?" asks Karamzin. His immediate answer is: "Because sparks of passionate love for mankind flash out in his very delusions; because his very weaknesses reveal some of his kindly good nature" (*SW*, II, 122).

Karamzin's poem *Darovaniya* (*Gifts*, 1796) is also a close parallel to his essay *Something about the Sciences*. . . . After describing the uncultured coarseness of primitive peoples, blind to the beauty of the world around them, the author relates how the muse of Fine Arts appeared among them:

> But suddenly Orpheus appeared
> With his melodious golden lyre,
> With ray of gifts from heavenly spheres . . .
> Whose charms with power radiant
> From souls dissolved all darkness dire:
> Set sparks of feeling bright ascending!
> For mortals a new age began:
> The Arts shone forth, all light transcending,
> On earth—And born anew was Man!
>
> (*CPW*, p. 215)

The ability to enjoy works of art, in the view of the poet, ennobles man and develops his sensitivity—the most precious quality from the standpoint of the Sentimentalist. Karamzin believed that if indeed people needed art, the artist must understand what kind of art. Believing that "the image of the creator [i.e., writer] is always found in the creation and often against his own will," Karamzin came to the conclusion that every author first and foremost "depicts the portrait of his own soul and heart" (*SW*, II, 120–21).

He drew attention to what he considered to be the most important thing in a work of art—the personality of its author—and developed his views on the arts and on the role of the poet-artist in some of his poems, particularly in *K bednomu poetu* (*To the Poor Poet*, 1796): "Reality, my friend, is poor: /Play in your soul with dreams and visions, / Or else life will be but a bore" (*CPW*, p. 193).

These lines are usually considered as evidence of Karamzin's increasing subjectivity due to his general spiritual crisis. Certainly, in this difficult period Karamzin's works show ever more clearly his desire to withdraw from the cruel and sad reality into a non-existent world created by his own imagination. However, the poem is far from introspective; it is permeated with light irony, and much of it refers to the poet himself and to his recent illusions. He writes:

> A poet has a wizard's craft:
> His thoughts—like elves, all magic staffed—
> Turn flower to Venus at command;
> Make pine to bloom with rose-red petal,
> Find tender myrtle in the nettle,
> Build castles out of grains of sand.

At the close of the poem, Karamzin asks, "What is a poet?" and comes to the conclusion:

> A poet? Apt liar his true name:
> Yet his the laurel wreath and fame.

The deception in the poem had also been a deception for the poet himself. Now that the poet realizes it, he is no longer an unintentional deceiver, but an "apt liar." The art lies in making the imagined seem probable and real. To do so, the poet must have a sound idea of reality:

> Who can construe a pleasant fiction
> Through prose or poetry—good luck!
> So long as it permits conviction.

> (*CPW*, p. 195)

Karamzin is somewhat of an absolutist regarding the subjective moment, unavoidable in the process of writing. However, in his view, the author is not at all separated from the real, objective world. His attitude to the world expresses those very qualities which give a man the right to be called a writer—kindness, the ability to enter into other people's sufferings, and "the holy, boundless desire for the general good, no matter in what sphere." In *What Is Necessary to the Author?*, Karamzin comes to the conclusion that "a wicked person cannot be a good author" (*SW*, II, 122).

In his attempt to unite concepts of the "good" and the "beautiful," Karamzin, like other Russian Sentimentalists, followed the esthetics developed by European enlighteners, such as Schiller. In Schiller's teachings, the Russian writer was undoubtedly attracted by the idea of man reaching perfection by developing a feeling for the beautiful.[14]

Similar ideas helped Karamzin regain a secure foothold in the treacherous period of his doubts and disappointments. His ethical values remained firm, and this served as the main argument of his Philalet, who appears once more several years later in Karamzin's essay *A Discourse on Happiness*.

The essay took the form of a dialogue: this time Philalet answers Melodor's questions in a lively conversation rather than by letter. As Philalet sets forth his reasoning, he is repeatedly interrupted by Melodor who finds more objections all the time. But Philalet has the last word, giving us cause to suppose that the views he expressed were more acceptable to the author. However, the doubts of Melodor, who represents Karamzin as the "second voice," are rather well founded.

Reflecting on "the means of being happy in one's life," Melodor asks in astonishment: "What do we work for? Why study, read, write, argue—and do, God knows what!—when we cannot find happiness in our life?"[15] Philalet admits that man cannot find "perfect bliss" on earth; but, in his opinion, everyone can "find many real gratifications in his life, need not be bored nor rile against fate, but be contented."[16] Melodor speaks of the numerous embitterments and anxieties that interfere with this. But Philalet has an answer to everything: he believes that only a man with a bad character can be really unhappy, because he is punished for the evil he does "by fate and by his own heart." Philalet finally concludes that "to be happy means to be kind."[17]

The ideas propagated by Philalet were not very new or original, but in Karamzin's interpretation they acquired an importance of unusual urgency for many Russian readers. The comforting philosophy of optimism enabled the writer to substantiate and strengthen his position in life during the years of political reaction, during the years when any attempt at restructuring society seemed meaningless and impossible. Being content with one's lot, which is what Philalet advocates, does not mean being completely passive. On the contrary, according to Philalet, man can be happy only if his kindness is directed into real action which benefits others.

Yet, Philalet's comfortable philosophy had its vulnerable spots: he does not discuss real people with their actual needs, passions, and sufferings, but talks of idealized creatures in the abstract. Philalet admits they might have passions, but in his opinion no fatal consequences could result, because the mind limits and guides acts of passion in the right direction.

However, examples from real life counteract this theory, and Karamzin himself in unison with Melodor could have objected to much that the well-intentioned Philalet said, and he continued to worry over the problem of the dependence of human destiny on the "will of fate" and on tragically complicated circumstances. During his spiritual crisis, this theme took on especially sharp outlines, which can be seen from a review of Karamzin's tales written during this period.

III   *New Tales*

> Creator! Why have you endowed people with the fatal power of bringing unhappiness to themselves and others?
>
> —N. M. Karamzin

Perhaps the most popular of all Karamzin's works published in the almanac *Aglaya* was his tale *Ostrov Borngolm (Bornholm Island)*. Its unusual and original plot fascinated the reader.

As in his previous tales, the writer pointed out that his story was "truth and not fancy." To make it more convincing, Karamzin details the circumstances of how he happened to hear the story. He refers to his tour of Europe which ended in England, and then tells what happened to him during his sea voyage from London to Russia.

The ship puts in at the small town of Gravesend, and here, on the seashore, the author meets a strange young man. His whole appearance reveals how unhappy he is. The stranger strums his guitar and sings a song that begins with these words:

> The laws condemn forever
> The object of my love—

> But who, Oh heart, may ever
> Against your passions move?

"Dear Bornholm" is mentioned in the song. It is linked with thoughts of his beloved Lila, but under a "parental curse" the young man has been banished from the shores of the island forever. Though excited by the song, the author does not have time to talk with the young stranger, since his ship is sailing out of Gravesend. But during the voyage, when the traveller finds himself just off Bornholm Island, he insists that the skipper give him a sloop, and he goes to the island. There he finds a gloomy castle and asks for shelter. The owner is an "honorable, grey-haired old man" on whose face the narrator sees "signs of a grieving heart." During the night, the traveller awakens and goes for a walk in the garden; following a path, he arrives at a cave. There, behind the iron bars of a dungeon, he sees a young woman who is slowly wasting away. The author addresses her with words of compassion and sympathy, but the recluse replies that she "kisses the hand which punishes her." Much shaken, the traveller leaves the cave and in the morning sees the owner, who has guessed what the visitor had seen during the night.

"We sat down under a tree," writes Karamzin, "and the old man told me a terrible story—a story you are not going to hear, my friends; it will keep for the next time. For now, I shall only say that I learned the secret of the Gravesend stranger: a dreadful secret!" (*SW*, I, 673).

This unexpected ending is not only a literary device, but also a forced measure of precaution. An alert reader could very easily have guessed the undisclosed secret: the guilty love of brother and sister who had been cursed and punished by their father. This version of the story is confirmed by material found in several manuscript collections dating from the end of the eighteenth century and the beginning of the nineteenth. In *Bornholm Island* one often comes across the song of the young man from Gravesend: "The laws condemn forever. . ." as an independent composition that has nothing to do with the text of the tale. In one of the manuscript collections a lengthy title explains the contents: "A song written by a brother pining away for his own sister, the former having been exiled by his father to a distant island."[18] In another collection, the text of the song is considerably changed, using the expression "sister-mistress." [19]

The tale excited not only the interest but the indignation of many readers. For instance, the poet and literary theoretician Semyon S. Bobrov wrote that "the delusion here is not in words, but in the feelings themselves! A sister-mistress! To justify the terrible voluptuousness of a brother for his sister by the laws of nature is as if it were in the first years of the golden age. . ."[20] However, similar plots were fairly common. Thus, it is less a question of Karamzin's borrowing the plot than that his tale parallels a number of works in European literature.

V. E. Vatsuro, who studied the question, pointed out that Karamzin's tale belongs integrally to the tradition of the so-called Gothic novel.[21] The very theme of incest and the separate motifs—incarcerating a woman in a dungeon, a mysterious castle, gloomy landscape—all bring *Bornholm Island* close to the works of Ann Radcliffe, Clara Reeve, Matthew Lewis, and other authors of Gothic fiction. However, the conflicts in Karamzin's tale serve to differentiate it materially from Gothic literature. Examining *Bornholm Island* in conjunction with other works from the almanac *Aglaya*, the critic reaches the conclusion that "the dialectic approach to the phenomena of the 'moral world,' which is the essential feature of the artistic method in *Bornholm Island,* is the direct result of an evolution in Karamzin's ideas."[22]

Conforming to the concept of a "sensitive person," the characters in *Bornholm Island* should arouse compassion rather than condemnation. Only "ruthless souls, cruel hearts" could reproach the passion of the young man from Gravesend; and the narrator is ready to rush up to the youth and press him to his heart. But the traveller also feels sympathy for the severe old man who gives him a friendly welcome and tries to overcome his grief. This man "loved virtue" but ended up deeply unhappy, in contradiction to the theory developed by Karamzin's Philalet in *A Discourse on Happiness*. However, the contradiction arising here is only imaginary, since all the complexity of the problem lies in what one understands virtue to be. To the old man's questions: "Does love still reign on earth? Is incense being burnt on the altars of virtue? Do the people prosper in countries you have seen?" the traveller answers: "The light of science is spreading more and more, but human blood still flows on earth; the tears of those in misery still fall; they praise the name of virtue, but argue about its essence"(*SW*, I, 668).

The tragic conflict of the tale is based on the confrontation of two different laws: on the one hand, the law of nature or law of "inborn feelings," and on the other, the "law of heaven" or the "law of the highest virtue."[23] The very concept of virtue becomes more complicated: "the virtuous old man," following the "laws of heaven," is forced to be stern and even cruel; he not only separates the lovers but makes Lila, his own daughter, a recluse in a dungeon. He breaks the "law of the heart," the law of nature, and this makes him a deeply unhappy man. The lovers were guilty before the "law of heaven," and so they are not virtuous. The old man also commits evil, commits a crime against the law of nature, and this deprives him of the right to be called virtuous.

Thus, the theme of all-powerful fate, met in the earlier works of Karamzin, becomes more acute in the tale of *Bornholm Island*. The characters created here are deeply tragic: they lack almost all the idyllic features typical of Sentimental heroes. Tense passions and gloomy mystery comprise the emotional atmosphere of this tale in which features of Romanticism may already be observed.

New literary tendencies were also reflected in another tale from the almanac *Aglaya—Sierra Morena*, which bears the subtitle *An Elegiac Extract from the Papers of N**.

The plot develops as follows: the hero, who tells the story, meets the beautiful Elvira in Andalusia. She is weeping over the loss of her fiancé, Alonso, who perished in a shipwreck. Trying to lighten Elvira's grief, the narrator spends long hours comforting her. He falls passionately in love with Elvira, but she has taken an oath not to love anyone but Alonso. However, gradually the narrator's passion is returned, and Elvira confesses her love. The lovers prepare for the wedding, but a moment before the ceremony a stranger appears, dressed in black, and reproaches Elvira for being unfaithful; he then stabs himself with a dagger. It is Alonso, who apparently had managed to be rescued. In despair, Elvira decides to spend the rest of her life in a convent. The narrator tells of long and sad wanderings, and of the peace that gradually came to his soul, for he has withdrawn from human society and lives in solitude.

The main source of the tale's plot was pointed out by the literary critic L. V. Krestova: the action develops similarly to that of an ancient Spanish ballad "About Brave Alonso and the Beautiful Imogene," which Matthew Lewis included in his novel *The Monk* (1795).[24] Karamzin worked out this plot in his own fashion, introducing many details which tie the tale integrally with his other works of the same period. One can even point to a certain auto-biographical trend in the tale, typical of most of the works published in the almanac *Aglaya*. The author's reflections on the vanity of human hopes and the impossibility of happiness are all directly connected with the inner crisis Karamzin was living through, having just lost his dearest friend and experiencing a sense of loneliness, not to speak of his confused despair over events taking place in Europe. The tale possibly reflects his disappointment over the outcome of the French Revolution and the resulting mood of skepticism which had permeated some lines in the correspondence between Melodor and Philalet, as well as certain poems and other works.

The work as a whole is distinctly marked with great emotional tension, and as a result the very manner of narration is not the same as in *Poor Liza* and *Natalya, the Boyar's Daughter*. It contains no particulars or details which might inform the reader about Elvira, Alonso, or the narrator himself. Their occupations, way of life, and social position do not interest the author. Turning away from concrete descriptions, he concentrates all his attention on depicting human passions and moods, and their constant shifting. This distinction gives the tale a poetical flavor, emphasized by the subtitle, *An Elegiac Extract*.

A special distinction of *Sierre Morena* is its picturesque, plastic images. It is enough to cite the opening passage as an example:

In flowering Andalusia, there where proud palm trees sway musically, where myrtle groves are aromatically fragrant, where majestic waters of the Guadalquivir slowly roll, where the Sierra Morena rises up crowned with rosemary—there, I saw the lovely one, when she stood, despondent and grieving, beside the monument to Alonso on which she rested her lily-white hand; a ray of the morning sun turned the white urn to gold and exalted the touching loveliness of tender Elvira, her light brown hair spilling down her shoulders and falling on the black marble. (*SW*, I, 674)

Brilliant colors are in sharp contrast: black mountain, lily-white hand, the ray of the sun that sheds gold, the white urn, light brown hair, black marble. As in the ballad *Raïsa,* a gamut of colors is created, harsh and unsoftened, which also conforms with the main theme of the tale—the confrontation of those tenderly and passionately in love with the insurmountable forces of fate. The first lines of the tale introduce an extraordinary world, a world of exotic nature and flaming passions. Even the sound effects are remarkable in the above extract. A certain rhythm is created by the repetition of similar grammatical constructions: four subordinate clauses beginning with the conjunction "where" are close in structure, the first two being almost exactly the same:

> where proud palm trees sway musically, where myrtle groves are aromatically fragrant. . . .

The repetition of the word "there" sharply changes the rhythmic design of what follows, and rings out like a struck chord introducing a new theme.

In his excited lyrical monologue, the narrator does not immediately call his beloved by name, nor does he even explain who Alonso is. It is far more important for the narrator to share the impression he has retained of his first meeting with Elvira.

Significantly, the narration is in the first person, and the narrator, differing from those in Karamzin's other tales, is not an observer sympathizing with the main characters, but the main participant in the events described. It is impossible to identify him with Karamzin, despite the remarks made referring to the tale as autobiographical. The narrator in *Sierre Morena* is a Romantic hero, bearing little resemblance to the author of the *Letters of a Russian Traveller*. The action is set in Andalusia—a country very exotic for Russian readers—Andalusia, where Karamzin had never been. Indications as to the truthfulness of the tale, so important for a Sentimental writer and present even in *Bornholm Island,* are utterly irrelevant here. In the main, the work exudes a far different character, no longer being a Sentimental tale, but one of the first tales of Russian Romanticism.

Bornholm Island and *Sierra Morena* were written by Karamzin during a time of intense inner crisis which laid its imprint on both works by showing the absolute helplessness of man before the will of fate and violent passions.

Gradually the writer overcame his crisis, and the skepticism and irony he had picked up from his "Agathon"—Petrov—again helped him through a difficult period. For the third issue of the almanac *Aglaya,* which never was published, Karamzin had written the tale *Julia,* where the theme of fate and the conflict between duty and emotion are given yet another interpretation. The tale came out in a separate edition in 1796, and its appearance marked a new and important stage in Karamzin's creative career as a prose writer.

The action takes place not in exotic, far away places, as in *Bornholm Island* and *Sierra Morena*, but in Moscow—in a social setting familiar both to Karamzin and to many of his readers. Young Julia, endowed with beauty and all possible virtues, attracts general attention in high society. Among her numerous admirers she singles out modest Aris. Then Prince N* makes an unexpected appearance in society; he is the "favorite of nature and fortune," and Julia is fascinated by him. The prince, though assuring Julia that he is passionately in love with her, definitely does not want to be tied down by getting married. He leaves Moscow, and Julia marries the faithful Aris; they leave "perfidious society" and settle down in a village. However, Julia soon tires of country life, and to please her, Aris brings her back to town. Soon the prince returns and begins visiting Julia's home. One time, Aris sees his wife and the prince on a garden path and overhears the prince declaring his love and talking of the need to follow "the call of the heart." At this moment Julia notices Aris, but he runs away and leaves Julia a letter of farewell. In despair, Julia parts with the prince and returns to the village, constantly reproaching herself and thinking of Aris. She bears Aris a son, Erast. Several years later, Aris unexpectedly returns and hears of Julia's faithfulness. Then follows the happy ending.

The heroine is faced with the same alternative as the lovers in *Bornholm Island*: "the law of the heart" or the "law of heaven." Julia undergoes the trial twice. The first time she does not yield to the temptations and assurances of the prince; the second time, pure chance comes to her aid in the sudden reappearance of Aris. The writer himself hints at a less happy outcome: "Julia—a hair's breadth from becoming a new Aspasia, another Raïsa—suddenly becomes an angel of chastity."[25] The author contrasts the behavior of Aris to what a Romantic hero would have done in his place; Aris does not rush at Julia and the prince with drawn dagger, but goes away quietly. The development of the plot has prepared the reader for a dramatic outcome, but at the peak of the climax the writer unexpectedly changes the course of events. Instead of a violent display of passion and bloodshed, everything is settled in an amicable way. The manner of narration corresponds to the plot development; the ironic tone, typical of Karamzin's early tales, but lacking in his Romantic writings, is particularly evident here.[26] In this respect, the image of the narrator has undergone a considerable change: there is no longer any sign of the "sensitive dreamer" —the author of *Poor Liza* and *Natalya, the Boyar's Daughter*—he is now a witty man of the world. Instead of a lyrical opening, typical of his early tales, the author plunges immediately into a conversation with the reader concerning who is better, man or woman. The story of Julia told by the narrator then illustrates the conversation. In the course of the narration, the heroine herself takes a most lively part in discussing this problem. Deserted by the prince, she attacks men; forgiven by Aris, she runs down women. The writer renders all this discussion with evident irony, softened somewhat by his sympathy for the heroine. The irony grows more serious when the discussion revolves around the opinions and laws of society and around the behavior of Prince N*.

Karamzin's tale was one of the first works to give a critical depiction of the customs and morals of high society. The range of themes of the Sentimental tale broadened; the possibility dawned of creating a new hero whose psychology would be determined by his social environment. The author's *Weltanschauung* grew more complex and artistically he grew more mature.

CHAPTER 5

The Messenger of Europe

I *A New Century and New Plans*

> ... The patriot and friend of the people will rejoice
> at seeing the light of intellect further and further
> crowding out the dark area of ignorance in Russia.
>
> —N. M. Karamzin

IN March 1801, Alexander I, son of Paul and grandson of Catherine the Great, ascended the throne. Most Russians regarded the event with sincere enthusiasm, placing great hopes in the young sovereign. It looked as though Alexander I would be a humane and enlightened ruler. The new Emperor was hailed in verse by such venerable poets as Kheraskov and Dmitriev, as well as by numerous second- and third-rate poets. The genre of the laudatory ode, which seemed to have outlived itself, suddenly came into general vogue again. Karamzin, who at one time had refused to write an ode to Catherine the Great, turned to it, too.

He wrote two odes: *To His Imperial Majesty Alexander I, Sovereign of All the Russias, on his Accession to the Throne* and *On the Solemn Coronation of His Imperial Majesty Alexander I, Sovereign of All the Russias*. However, these works did not express his loyalty as a subject or a desire to ingratiate himself with the monarch. In the best traditions of the Russian Classical ode, Karamzin used this genre to state his social and political program, presented to the Tsar in cleverly veiled form. Alexander I was only twenty-three years old; nothing could be said of his past services—for him, everything lay ahead, in the future. This was an especially important moment for Karamzin. The summit of good had no ceiling:

> You can do all—you still are young!
>
> (*CPW*, p.262)

The poet wanted the Emperor to become "the sun of enlightenment," a kind and just sovereign, a condemner of base flattery and instigations.

Alexander accepted Karamzin's verses very favorably, and this, coupled with the first liberal reforms, served as an excuse for certain illusions the writer entertained about the rule of the new Emperor. The experience he had gained from the French Revolution confirmed Karamzin's conviction that a firm state power based on law was necessary and even salutary for the people. From his point of view, the only suitable form of such power for Russia lay in a monarchy. The writer had lived during the reigns of Catherine the Great and Paul I, and neither of these sovereigns, in his opinion, had been a monarch who could be the examplar for the young Emperor. But since the ideal did not exist in reality, Karamzin had to picture it in his own imagination and, for plausibility, attach it to the name of a real person. Paul I—murdered in a conspiracy inspired by the enmity and even hatred of many people close to the heir apparent Alexander—could not serve as a felicitous example. It was quite a different matter with Catherine the Great, who had in her time given much attention and care to her eldest grandson. In addition, her reign was now somewhat removed with the passing of time, and Alexander I—only a boy when she ruled—knew many things only from hearsay. For this reason, Karamzin wrote his work *Istoricheskoe pokhvalnoe slovo Ekaterine II (A Historic Word of Praise to Catherine II,* 1802).

Naturally, those sad times when his close friends, Novikov and other Masons, were persecuted could not be erased from Karamzin's memory, but the purpose of this eulogy to Catherine was to depict an ideal image of a sovereign worthy of imitation. Karamzin wanted to make Catherine's lofty ideas, which had existed only in her words, an immediate guide to action for Alexander I. Therefore, Karamzin persistently stated that "earthly sovereigns must rule for the benefit of the people."[1]

The first years of the reign of Alexander, who tried to win trust and love, were quite auspicious for literary activities. Karamzin was quick to see this, and in 1802 he again turned to journalism. *Vestnik Evropy (The Messenger of Europe)* was the title of the new journal he published. It lasted for a long time—to 1830. Karamzin was publisher and editor only from 1802 to the end of 1803, but during his tenure the journal gained enormous popularity with Russian and foreign readers. When he resigned his post on the journal, Karamzin wrote in the last issue of 1803 that "*The Messenger* has been fortunate in having earned a flattering reputation among foreign writers; many Russian works taken from the journal have been translated into German and French and have appeared in journals published in these languages."[2]

As time went on, the character of the journal changed with each new publisher, editor, and selection of contributors.[3] As for Karamzin, publishing *The Messenger of Europe* marked a time that revealed new aspects of his literary talent.

The first years of the new century brought important changes, not only in Russian social and political life, but in Karamzin's personal affairs as well. In 1801, he married Elizaveta Protasova, the sister of Anastasia Pleshcheeva, with whom he had long been friends. Tender and loving relations existed between husband and wife, but their life together was all too short. On April 4, 1802, soon after the birth of their daughter, Sophia, the writer's wife died. Karamzin was terribly shocked by the tragedy; yet, despite his grief he continued to work persistently and intensively.

The Messenger of Europe, a bimonthly, demanded much of his strength and energy because Karamzin himself wrote most of the articles, as he had for the *Moscow Journal*. However, there was an essential difference between the two periodicals:[4] a completely new section under the heading "Politics" was introduced in *The Messenger of Europe*. The remaining material—original and translated tales, articles, verses, and so on—was included in a section called "Literature and Miscellany." Works published in the latter were by Dmitriev, Derzhavin, Kheraskov, Neledinski-Meletsky, and others. In one of the issues Karamzin published a poem by Zhukovsky, *A Country Churchyard*—a free translation of Thomas Gray's famous *Elegy Written in a Country Churchyard*—one of the first examples of Romanticism in Russian literature.

The Messenger carried some of Karamzin's new verses, diverse in character as usual, including the ironic *Gimn Gluptsam* (*Hymn to Fools*) and an elegiac verse *Melankholiya—Podrazhenie Delilyu* (*Melancholy—in Imitation of Delille* [Jacques Delille, 1738–1813]), one of the most interesting examples of Russian philosophical lyrics of the early nineteenth century. There was also the poem *Bereg* (*The Shore*), devoted to the theme of life and death. But it was undoubtedly prose that was most prominently featured in the journal. Karamzin also published some of his original tales, which were of extreme importance for his creative career. Some of his articles discussed contemporary political events, others were devoted to domestic affairs (agriculture, education, book selling, culture) and what had always engrossed Karamzin—problems of literature and language. Considerable space was also devoted to historical articles.

The writer continued translating extensively for the journal, and *The Messenger of Europe* carried his translations of Mme de Genlis, La Fontaine, and other European writers. In addition, he looked through a great number of foreign journals and newspapers, selected what he considered the most important articles, and translated and published some in every issue. Once Karamzin wrote: "Leaving it to the publishers of *The News* (*Vedomosti*) to report all kinds of political items in brief, we shall concentrate only on important news, and *The Messenger of Europe,* as a collection of issues, may then form a select library of literature and politics" (*SW*, II, 268). The Russian reader thus received the latest information about events taking place in Europe, as well as in America and Asia. The selection supplied by Karamzin was usually distinguished by its thoughtful approach, the material was always versatile, translations were exact, and every article retained a high literary style. However, the translation of newspaper texts presented certain difficulties, because for certain social and economic concepts no comparable words existed in Russian. In such cases, Karamzin often introduced loan words from the foreign language, using the words in the same figurative sense they had in the original language. Sometimes the writer himself created new words, for example, the word *promyshlennost*—"industry." As a rule, these words easily took root in Russian, mainly due to Karamzin's particularly subtle feeling for the language.

Among all the journals of that time, *The Messenger of Europe* stands out for its wealth of contents and for retaining a consistently even style. Not surprisingly, therefore, it enjoyed a success equal to that of its predecessor, the *Moscow Journal.*

The second edition of the *Moscow Journal,* which Karamzin again published through 1801 and 1802, and which sold out quickly, also demanded a considerable amount of work. Regular readers of Karamzin's publications grew in number with each year, and the writer's fame became generally recognized. The natural result of Karamzin's literary success was the publication of his first collected works in eight volumes, later in nine, in 1803–04 and 1814, respectively.

Meanwhile, new ideas and plans were ripening in Karamzin's mind. His long interest in the history of his fatherland noticeably came to a head during the years he was publishing *The Messenger of Europe*. It was in this period that Karamzin began preparing and collecting material for his seminal long-range work, the *History of the Russian State*. It was a time in his life which he considered to be the happiest.

II *From Literature to Politics and from Politics to Literature*

> Literature, contributing more to true enlightenment
> than ever before, now turned to confirming all kinds
> of social relations.
>
> —N. M. Karamzin

Although political articles in *The Messenger of Europe* concerning contemporary international life were allotted a special section by Karamzin, they were actually very closely related to other materials published under the heading "Literature and Miscellany." Generalizations were made on a factual basis and were reflected, either directly or indirectly, in Karamzin's publicistic works and fiction written during the same period.

Karamzin suffered over the collapse of his youthful illusions and his disappointment in the French Revolution, but he continued to follow closely the development of events in France.[5] In his "General Review," which opened the political section in the first issue of *The Messenger of Europe*, he states with satisfaction that "France, despite being called a Republic and [despite] certain reforms in its rule, is now in fact nothing more than an out-and-out monarchy" (*SW*, II, 262). Karamzin's sympathetic attitude toward Napoleon can be assessed from the items featured in *The Messenger*, both those from foreign publications and his own articles. Karamzin called Napoleon a "Monarch-Councillor"; that is, he did not attach special significance to his real title. For him, the most important matter was the policy pursued by the head of the French state. Karamzin wrote about Napoleon: "He, of course, deserves the gratitude of Frenchmen. He will give the Republic a wise system of civil laws, he will be a sincere sponsor of the sciences, arts, trade; and on this foundation he will build up France's prosperity, using a policy of peace to coordinate her interests with those of other countries" (*SW*, II, 265).

In his article "Priyatnye vidy, nadezhdy i zhelaniya nyneshnego vremeni" ("Pleasant Aspects, Hopes and Desires of the Present Time") Karamzin expressed his opinion of the benefits brought about by the Revolution: The revolutionary experiment has proven that "civil order is sacred even in its most localized or subsidiary deficiencies; that its power is not tyranny for the people, but a defense against tyranny" (*SW*, II, 268–69). Anarchy—in his opinion the most damaging consequence of the Revolution—aroused sharply negative feelings in Karamzin. Any form of rule, he felt, even tyranny, was better for the people than complete anarchy and the absence of any laws.

Karamzin felt sympathetic toward the ideas which had inspired the French revolutionaries; the idea of common brotherhood and general prosperity still attracted him.[6] To Karamzin, a republic was "an ideal, inaccessible but captivating dream."[7] However, the implementation of this dream into actual practice led to something quite different from what Karamzin had expected.

In his eyes, the establishment of a republican system in France had entailed bloodshed, numberless victims, and unwarranted cruelty, but he was not satisfied with the results of the Revolution. Its participants had apparently not been prepared to solve problems which Karamzin considered of primary importance. He believed that every true citizen of a republic must possess exceptionally high moral qualities, but such a utopian view was hardly practical. Therefore, he thought it was necessary to find other less direct but more realistic means of securing as many social and political benefits for society as possible.

Considering that a monarchy would perhaps be the most convenient form of rule, he did not idealize it, but accepted the need for it, albeit with reservations, as the lesser evil compared to anarchy, being fully aware of the possibility of a dangerous transition from monarchy to despotism. While sympathizing with Napoleon, Karamzin nevertheless published in *The Messenger of Europe* an article by Camille Jourdain entitled "The Real Meaning of the People's Agreement to the Perpetual Tenure of Napoleon Bonaparte as Premier Consul," in which the author upheld the idea that "peace and order" were not sufficient for national prosperity, that the people desired to "contribute to the establishment of such an order, to safeguard it, [and] to be happy according to their own ideas and not those of others." "How terrible," exclaimed Karamzin, the publicist, "to base the happiness of a whole people on the perishable thread of one man's life!"[8] Similar ideas seemed rather interesting and important to Karamzin; by introducing them to the Russian reader, he displayed his independence and also a certain boldness with regard to the government of Alexander I.

Karamzin, who affirmed the advantages of monarchy and sincerely regretted the execution of the French king, always pointed to republican leaders as worthy examples to follow. One cannot fail to observe the number of articles in the *The Messenger of Europe* dealing with the United States of America and the American Revolution.[9] The writer was primarily concerned with the results and the consequences of this revolution, which seemed to him completely different from those in France. The "Letters from the United States of America" which Karamzin published dealt with the progressive character of the republican government,[10] and in the opinion of the author, the American people owed this progressiveness to Thomas Jefferson, "faithful executor of laws" and "ardent republican." Another article was devoted to the positive qualities of George Washington.

The leaders of the American Revolution undoubtedly attracted Karamzin because of their highly moral personal qualities and their loyalty to the interests of their people. Such features never failed to arouse the writer's respect, no matter what nation a man belonged to, nor what power he possessed. In this connection, Karamzin's journal printed a piece of news taken from an American newspaper, *The Salem Gazette,* about a Negro named Caesar, once chief of an African tribe, who had fallen into slavery, had been sold to an American merchant, and finally had escaped, living in the woods with his companions and winning wide fame as "a noble brigand" ("King Caesar, a Negro in America").[11]

Karamzin also acquainted his readers with a number of other Americans. For instance, *The Messenger of Europe* carried "The Letter of Don Joachimo Garcia, Governor of the Spanish-owned island of Santo Domingo, to the President of the United States of America,"[12] expressing gratitude to an American captain for having rescued people from a Spanish ship wrecked during a storm.

However, Karamzin was not at all inclined to idealize the New World. The articles devoted to the United States contained material revealing various aspects of life. For example, one article spoke unfavorably about the spirit of business and trade which flourished in America and about the urge for riches whose importance crowded out all other interests.

For Karamzin, the United States was not an exotic country of fairy tale character, but a fully realistic one, and his attention was drawn to its state structure and the customs and mores of its inhabitants. As a result, the information the writer presented, no matter how fragmentary, permitted Russian readers of the time to get to know something of American life.[13]

Karamzin, as publisher of *The Messenger of Europe*, kept the interest in the culture, customs, morals, and characters of peoples of different nations that he had acquired in his youth and which he displayed in the *Letters of a Russian Traveller* and his articles in the *Moscow Journal*. Now, Karamzin felt a deeper and a more distinct need to define the special features of the Russian character and turned to the history and culture of his own country, as did many other men of letters who were also becoming increasingly aware of the development of national consciousness in Russian society.

Karamzin, with his knowledge of European life and culture, could approach the most urgent contemporary problems from a broad, historical perspective. Witness for instance his article "On Love for the Fatherland and National Pride," one of the most significant works to appear in *The Messenger of Europe*.

In this article, Karamzin affirms that patriotism "demands reasoning—and therefore, not all people possess it" (*SW*, II, 282). He distinguishes three kinds of patriotic love: "Physical"—attachment to the place of one's birth and upbringing; "moral"—love for one's countrymen; and "political"—which Karamzin understood as "love for the well-being and glory of one's fatherland, and the desire to further it in all spheres" (*SW*, II, 280ff). The writer continues by giving a concrete definition of his understanding of "well-being" and "glory." Turning to Russia's past, he mentions examples of the courage and fortitude of Russians who succeeded in taking a stand for their national independence. However, of no less importance than military victories were the achievements won by the Russian people in the area of enlightenment, since the well-being—the good of a country—Karamzin was convinced, depends on the degree of its enlightenment. Rejecting false patriotism, based on the assumption that "we are better than everybody in everything," the writer further developed his idea: "Let us accept that some nations are in general more enlightened than we, because their circumstances have been more favorable; but let us also keep in mind all the intellectual benefits fate has blessed the Russian people with; let us take our place boldly in line with the rest, pronounce our name clearly, and repeat it with noble pride" (*SW*, II, 282–83).

Considering that "imitativeness" was not a drawback but rather a worthy quality in the Russian character, Karamzin mentions how quickly Russia was able to make use of what European science and art had achieved, and make such advances in the field of enlightenment that "others could and must learn from us." The writer attaches special importance to the development of literature, regarding it as a manifestation of people's enlightenment on the one hand, and as a means of spreading enlightenment on the other. Karamzin believed that literature was a matter of great social significance. Proceeding from this assumption, he attempted to attract readers to books in the Russian language. At the same time he realized the complexity of this problem, for educated people in Russian society had long been bound by the habit of speaking French. Karamzin took a decisive stand against preference for a foreign language over the native tongue and spoke of the merits and rich possibilities of Russian. He considered that the development and perfection of the Russian language was a task of major importance facing Russian writers of his time.

The ideas expressed in the article represented a summary of all Karamzin's past beliefs and at the same time were his program for the future. His reflections on his publishing and creative work were inseparable from his meditations over Russia's destiny. Still a confirmed champion of enlightenment, Karamzin believed as before that the dissemination of knowledge, humanistic culture in particular, was the most reliable road to universal prosperity.

His publicistic article "O lyubvi k otechestvu i narodnoy gordosti" ("On Love for the Fatherland and National Pride") was supplemented by several others published in *The Messenger of Europe*, such as "O knizhnoy torgovle i lyubvi ko chteniyu v Rossii" ("On the Book Trade and Love for Reading in Russia"), and "Otchego v Rossii malo avtorskikh talantov?" ("Why Is There Little Writing Talent in Russia?"). The problem of the reader and the reader's perceptive ability, of particular concern to Karamzin, was fully and seriously discussed in these articles—as a social problem. The writer was interested not only in the number of book shops, their trade turnover, the number of subscribers to newspapers, and buyers of books, but also in the social strata to which readers belonged. Karamzin asserted that "it is true that many of the gentry, even those who are well off, do not take newspapers, but merchants and people of the lower middle class more than make up for it: they like to read them. The very poorest people subscribe, and the most illiterate want to know what is written from foreign lands!" (*SW*, II, 177).

He found the question of readers' tastes and needs exceptionally important—what books were in greatest demand, what the readers liked, and what kind of readers they were. From his observations he concluded that in Russia novels were read more than anything else; even a person untrained and unaccustomed to reading could find fiction congenial and interesting. Karamzin was also concerned about the reader's grasp of literature and concluded that "as long as there is too wide a gap between author and reader, the first, no matter how clever, cannot have very much influence on the latter" (*SW*, II, 179). Karamzin never lost sight of this, for no matter what he wrote about or what genre he turned to, he always kept in mind the needs and tastes of his readers, and not only as a personal writing guide, but also as a means of elevating and improving the morals of the reading public.

III   *The Evolution of the "Sensitive" Hero*

> Not everybody is capable of philosophizing or of putting himself in the shoes of the story's protagonists; but everybody is either presently in love, has been in love, or wants to be in love, and therefore discovers his very own self in the Romantic hero.
>
> —N. M. Karamzin

By the time Karamzin had begun publishing *The Messenger of Europe,* the genre of the Sentimental tale had already taken on a clear-cut form and was firmly established in Russian literature. One of the literary plots in popular favor was still Karamzin's *Poor Liza* or variations on it, and this meant the emergence of certain more or less stereotyped main characters in tales hardly less stereotyped: "a sensitive" heroine who suffered because of an unfaithful lover; "a villain" who deceived the heroine; and a "sensitive" author who sympathized with her. But, despite their tendency to moralize, Russian authors of Sentimental tales gradually gave up the absolute ethical criteria typical of Classicism and accepted moral values that were more elastic. An important role in this process was played by the influence of works by Sterne, Wieland, Moritz, and other European authors who strove to discover the complex psychology governing man; and with his understanding and knowledge of contemporary European literature, Karamzin managed to avoid one-sidedness in depicting a "seducer" even as early as in *Poor Liza*.

As for Karamzin's evolving *Weltanschauung* and creative development, while publishing *The Messenger of Europe* he set new artistic aims for himself.[14] In the first decade of the nineteenth century, his writings concerned psychological problems which he solved on a new, higher level. This is particularly true of the tales published in *The Messenger of Europe: Moya ispoved* (*My Confession*, 1802(, *Chuvstvitelny i kholodny* (*The Sensitive Man and the Cold Man*, 1803) *Rytsar nashego vremeni* (*A Knight of Our Times*, 1803).

The not very lengthy *My Confession* is a story told by Count N. N. about his life. Born into a rich, noble family, he received the most fashionable education: he "learned French, but did not know his mother tongue," and "at the age of fifteen had no conception as to the proper duties expected of a man or citizen" (*SW*, I, 730). To continue his education, he was sent abroad in the company of Hofmeister Mendel, who was not only ignorant as a tutor, but a schemer who tried to get all the personal benefits possible from his job. The hero spends three idle years in Leipzig, then sets out on a tour of Europe. The count seeks amusement everywhere, becomes entangled in many love affairs, and drinks so much that he finally has to stay in bed.

On returning to Russia, he feels he has become a leading figure of fashion: "Everywhere I went I saw myself from top to toe as if in a mirror, my every gesture was copied and repeated with utter faithfulness" (*SW*, I, 733). The count is very successful with women and is amused if he manages to separate husband from wife or come between two close girl friends. When he finally marries Emilia, who is not rich, he immediately proves unfaithful and introduces his wife to the morals of worldly society. Endless balls, the theater, and dinner parties ruin the count; he becomes penniless and is threatened with debtors' prison. At this point a wealthy prince asks him to sign certain documents giving the prince the right to marry Emilia. The count consents, but in the back of his mind he has other plans. In the prince's house later on, he seduces his former wife, causing scandalous notoriety. Though reunited with Emilia, the count is again unfaithful, and continues having love affairs after she dies. He becomes a money-lender and pimp who is received "in many distinguished families."

With good reason, critics saw in *My Confession* a unique parody of certain works by Rousseau (*The Confession* and *Émile*). Yet, it was not a parody designed to make fun of Rousseau's ideas, but to confirm them by using the "rule of contraries."

Count N. N. laughs at writers who use their novels to describe "the life of the heart"—a theme Karamzin always regarded as important. Was this, then, a complete renunciation of his former views and convictions? To answer, one must establish whether the opinions of the tale's hero coincide with those of the author and, if they do, to what extent.

A good part of *My Confession* is devoted to drawing a satirical picture of the morals of worldy society. Yet Karamzin does not moralize; instead, his hero assumes the role of critic and accuser and even tries to show how environment has influenced him. Summing up his life, the count refuses to accept the rebukes and scorn of "certain people," declaring: "But [why] should I believe them when I see, on the other hand, how many of our dear compatriots try to imitate me, live without aim, marry without love, divorce for fun, and bring themselves to ruin for the sake of giving dinner parties?" (*SW*, I, 739).

One can hear Karamzin's voice in these words, a Karamzin revolted by the senselessness and futility of society life.

The hero of the tale is not a primitive, simple soul; he is no fool, but is perfectly aware of the vulgarity of the world around him. However, he is unable to resist this world and therefore adjusts himself to it, while inwardly despising it. His boredom is frequently mentioned in the tale. All the evil he does and his seemingly senseless and wild behavior are only ways of adding spice to life. Thus, kissing the shoe of the Pope, the hero "bit his foot, making the poor old man scream at the top of his lungs." Though it amuses the hero only momentarily, this joke gives him much enjoyment.

Karamzin was very bold in endowing his hero with individual traits that could be taken as autobiographical; but the author and the hero are entirely disparate personalities. The hero is a cynic lacking in spiritual values; the author is an active "enlightener"— one who keeps believing in the goodness of man's nature and in the possibility of his moral perfection.[15]

In his psychological sketch *The Sensitive Man and the Cold Man*, Karamzin used another technique to depict the "sensitive" hero. The plot is of secondary importance, the chief intention being to depict two opposite characters.

Erast and Leonid had been friends from their youth, but even then they exhibited diametrically opposed traits of character: Erast—enthusiastic, ardent, and emotional; Leonid—sober, sensible, and cold. When Erast marries, his wife, Nina, falls in love with Leonid who, out of pure common sense, goes away to avoid trouble. However, when Erast finds himself in the same situation, he is not strong enough to resist the emotion he feels for his friend's wife and stops his visits only when Leonid, as master of his house, orders him out. "Cold" Leonid proves to be more virtuous than "sensitive" Erast, and Karamzin censures neither one nor the other, but merely seeks to understand the specifics of each character. Although the author cannot conceal his sympathy for Erast, who is more like himself and therefore easier to understand, he also finds features in Leonid that are likeable. He does not identify himself directly with either hero, views both with detachment, and tries to remain utterly impartial and objective.

A different relationship exists between author and protagonist in Karamzin's third tale, *A Knight of Our Times*. First conceived as a novel, the intention was not realized, and the work remained incomplete with only a lightly sketched plot conflict.

In the introduction, the author informs the reader of his intention "to tell a romantic story about a friend of his" (*SW*, I, 755). He gives a detailed account of the childhood of his protagonist, Leon, whose father was a retired "Russian nobleman of an old local family" living on the family estate on the banks of the Volga. Leon's mother, a pensive lady inclined to melancholy, died when the boy was seven, but her image had never left his heart. Quick to learn to read and write, Leon does a lot of reading, mostly of novels from his mother's library. After a few years, a certain Count Mirov and his beautiful young wife, Emilia, settle on a neighboring estate. Emilia is very sweet to the boy. To Leon, she resembles his mother, and a tender relationship develops between them. The narration breaks off at

Chapter Thirteen which describes how little Leon plays the role of "a new Actaeon" by watching Emilia bathing.

Leon's adventures are described in an amused, ironic tone, but with a different shade of irony than that used in *My Confession*. If one could call Count N. N. the antithesis of the sensitive hero, then Leon combines the nobleness of the sensitive hero with the weaknesses and even vices of the hero's antithesis.

The life story of the boy hero in *A Knight of Our Times* contains many episodes and circumstances taken from Karamzin's own life. Certainly Leon is very much akin to the author, both in character and in the way he looks at the world. Yet, a considerable distance lies between them: a gap in time above all. The author is a mature person rich in life experience. Leon is a child who resembles the author in childhood, but not the adult author. Thus, the narration develops along two planes: Leon's perception of events, and their interpretation by the mature author. Karamzin mentions this dual aspect of the narrative: "I must look at things only through the eyes of my hero" (*SW*, I, 782), he says, setting himself against those novelists who write of things that smack of unreality. The writer tries to reveal the inner world of each character by adopting his point of view, trying "to see with his eyes" and think his thoughts.

Both Leon and Emilia are as "sensitive" as Karamzin, but their inner world is noticeably unlike the author's. Thus, the concept of "sensibility" takes on a change of meaning: it is no longer of a one-dimensional positive character, but a psychologically intricate and complex one. The tale, therefore, stops being "Sentimental" in the true meaning of the word, and draws closer to the psychological worldy tale which was developed in Russian literature during the subsequent decades of the nineteenth century.

IV *A Historical Tale*—Marfa-posadnitsa

> When showing a foreigner the worthy images of our ancient heroes, a Russian would talk to him about their deeds; and the foreigner would want to read our chronicles.
>
> —N. M. Karamzin

The tale *Marfa-posadnitsa, ili Pokorenie Novagoroda (Martha the Mayoress, or, The Subjugation of Novgorod)* has a special place in

Karamzin's literary works published in *The Messenger of Europe*. The historical theme which had appeared in Karamzin's earlier works (*Poor Liza, Natalya, the Boyar's Daughter, Letters of a Russian Traveller*) takes precedence here and determines the character of the tale.

In 1803 Karamzin published an article entitled "Information on Marfa-posadnitsa, Taken from the Life of Saint Zosima," which describes Marfa as one of the most remarkable women in Russian history. In it he mentions the fairy tale printed in *The Messenger of Europe*—that is, Karamzin's own tale of the same name. Both the tale and the article are based on the same historical fact.

In the preface to the tale Karamzin made it clear that fantasy played an important role in the work: "By chance I came across an ancient manuscript which I am now going to relate to lovers of history and of fairy tales, touching up the style only where it is obscure and unintelligible" (*SW*, I, 680).

Thus, the writer interprets the subtitle, *A Historical Tale,* as a fairy tale, yet based on true historical events. "All the main events coincide with history," Karamzin emphasized, and this is what makes *Marfa-posadnitsa* essentially different from *Natalya, the Boyar's Daughter,* which was more of a fairy tale than a historical tale.

The action takes place at the end of the fifteenth century. The Moscow Prince, Ioann (Ivan III), wants to annex the independent republic of Novgorod and sends Prince Kholmsky there to negotiate. Making a clever, eloquent speech, Kholmsky tries to persuade the people of Novgorod to submit to Ivan. Marfa-posadnitsa—the mayoress elected by the town's Popular Assembly—follows with her speech before the Assembly. Hers is a much more impassioned and lively oration about the advantages of freedom which Novgorodians enjoy and the miserable lot of those who have lost their liberty. Marfa's words have a decisive effect upon the people, and Novgorod declares war on Ivan. Marfa then recommends Miroslav as army commander; he is a handsome, courageous young man, and Marfa decides to give him her daughter, Xenia, in marriage. In the name of Novgorod, Marfa writes a letter to the city of Pskov asking for support.

Meanwhile, solemn wedding celebrations are held for Miroslav and Xenia, and Marfa tells her daughter how much she once loved her husband, Isaac Boretsky, who perished in the war with the

Lithuanians, stressing that she had given him her oath to defend the liberty of Novgorod. No help comes from Pskov, but the Novgorodians boldly go into battle against the Muscovite army, which is superior in number. Miroslav shows exceptional daring but is killed in battle, and Ivan proves victorious. Stubbornly, Marfa urges the Novgorodians to keep fighting against the stronger enemy, calling on them to die for the sake of liberty. Novgorod refuses to surrender, though starvation is rampant in the besieged town. At last, in a final battle, the people of Novgorod lose and Ivan enters with his troops. Marfa fearlessly awaits execution and mounts the scaffold with the words: "Subjects of Ivan! I die a citizen of Novgorod! . . . " In Ivan's name, Kholmsky promises the townspeople mercy and prosperity.

Karamzin does not adhere to historical facts on every point and is fully aware of it. Comparing this tale with corresponding sections in the *History of the Russian State,* critics have pointed out a number of discrepancies.[16] For example, in the *History*, Karamzin states that Marfa died in a convent, while in the tale she heroically goes to her execution. Karamzin considered deviations from the facts quite permissible in a tale addressed to lovers of fairy tales. He permitted himself even greater freedom in depicting the characters of the historical personages—Marfa, Ivan, and others. It was important to Karamzin to show them not as they were in reality, but the way he wished to see them; these images personified the writer's concept of ideal political figures.

Karamzin's Marfa is the ideal of civic virtue. Like the legendary women of Rome, she accepts the news stoically when told that her sons have died for their fatherland. Throughout the story, Marfa is surrounded by a halo of grandeur; in triumph and defeat, she conducts herself with firmness and independence. The epithets Karamzin applies to Marfa are important: she goes to address the people "calmly and majestically"; Marfa is "a majestic woman"; the people are moved by her "magnanimity"; kneeling before the people, she commits a "magnanimous act of humiliation"; she gazes on the citizens, before her execution, with "majestic despondency."

The writer shows how Marfa is regarded by the people: "the people demanded wise, magnanimous, courageous Marfa." As a parallel, he cites the words of Marfa's enemies who "dared to call her cruel, ambitious, and inhuman." However, both appraisals are based on more or less outward signs of Marfa's character. For

Karamzin—the author of psychological tales—such an appraisal
was insufficient; he wanted to show the deep underlying reasons
that determined Marfa's conduct. Therefore, he has his heroine tell
Xenia and Miroslav her story, which is almost a confession. Marfa
admits that when she was young she was not made for strength or
heroism. She "lived only for her husband and family in the quietness
of her home, was afraid of noisy crowds, and walked through the
public squares [*po stognam*] only to go to the sacred temples..."
(*SW*, I, 703). But love for her husband, "the virtuous hero who lived
and breathed for his fatherland," changed Marfa's character and
way of life. After the death of Isaac Boretsky, she became a new person: "with bold firmness she presided over the Council of Elders,"
"spoke at the Veche" (the Popular Assembly), and "moved the
people to surge like the sea; demanded war and bloodshed" (*SW*,
I, 703). The secret source of this transformation was love, and all
of Marfa's actions, judged so differently by friend and foe, were the
result of this deep emotion. In the introduction Karamzin comments
on this feature of Marfa's character when speaking of the imaginary
author of the manuscript whose contents he is supposedly relating:
"The secret motivation which he [i.e., the author of the manuscript]
attributes to Marfa's fanaticism, proves that he saw in her only a
passionate, ardent, and clever woman, but not a great and virtuous
one" (*SW*, I, 681).

Attempting to show the reader the inner motives of the heroine's
actions, Karamzin continued to develop the psychological line
which had occupied such a major place in his other tales. *Marfa-
posadnitsa* is not a Sentimental tale. Its very theme—the struggle
of the Novgorodians for their independence—puts this work closer
to the genre of Classicism. A certain antiquated style intensifies this
resemblance and, as has been observed, "Karamzin's 'Classicism'
in *Marfa-posadnitsa* is a peculiar parallel to the Classicism in the
tragedies of Marie Joseph Chénier, in the elegies of André Chénier,
in the paintings of David." [17] As for Russian Classicial works, which
by and large have little in common with Karamzin's tale, it is
interesting to recall the tragedy *Vadim of Novgorod* by Yakov B.
Knyazhnin, published in 1793, and recognized as an extraordinarily
bold political work, even bordering on sedition. Its plot was also
based on an episode taken from Russian history: the struggle of the
Novgorod ruler Vadim against the despotic rule of Prince Ryurik.

Though defeated, Vadim dies in the knowledge of his moral superiority over Ryurik. He tells the latter before stabbing himself:

> In the midst of your victorious army,
> Crowned, mightier than all you see at your feet —
> What are you, compared with one who dares to die?[18]

With similar feelings, Marfa goes to her execution; like Vadim, she is dedicated to the idea of liberty. In his tale, Karamzin repeatedly brings in the name of Vadim, whom he regards as the symbol of free Novgorod. The Popular Assemblies take place in the square bearing his name (Vadimovo mesto) where a marble statue of Vadim stands. Addressing the Novgorodians, Marfa says with pride that her ancestors were friends of Vadim and calls on Vadim to witness her love for her native city and her native land; like Vadim, she wishes to give the hand of her daughter to a man who will take up the cause of Novgorod's freedom. But, where Knyazhnin's work had been considered dangerous and pernicious because of its anti-monarchical content and had long been banned by tsarist censorship, the fate of *Marfa-posadnitsa* was quite another matter. And it is not surprising, because even with Karamzin's sympathy for the Novgorod republic, he was still resolved to show the historical inevitability of its annihilation. As a result, Ivan, the subjugator of Novgorod, is pictured, not as a cruel conqueror, but as a wise and noble ruler thinking about the interests of Russia as a whole. The idea of a united Russian state was regarded by Karamzin as correct and progressive, historically speaking. Although he arouses admiration for Marfa's heroism, the writer finds it important to explain that "the secret source" of her strength is not wisdom, but passion.

As in several of Karamzin's earlier works, such as *The Graveyard* or the correspondence of Philalet and Melodor, two voices resound throughout the tale of *Marfa-posadnitsa*, expressing two opposite points of view, yet each in its way having an affinity to the author. Is he a republican or a champion of monarchy? This question seems to be posed rather sharply in this tale, yet no direct answer is given. In the introduction it is said of the author that "the blood of Novgorod apparently runs in his blood"; however, the resistance of the Novgorodians is called imprudent. Just as before, a republic remains for Karamzin only a dream, an unattainable ideal. He looks upon monarchy as a reality which must be condoned for the sake of a supreme purpose—for Russia's welfare. As Karamzin imagines it, Ivan knows better than Marfa what constitutes this welfare; therefore, his victory is in the order of things. The writer tried to show that Marfa's stubbornness was a tragic delusion and that the interests of the Novgorodians were, in reality, inseparable from the interests of all the Russian people.

Karamzin emphasized the heroism and stoic firmness of Marfa, Xenia, Miroslav, and other Novgorodians, but stressed that these qualities were inherent in them as Slavs and as Russians. Describing the decisive battle, he remarked: "Glorious and great deeds! Only Russians could fight so, on both sides; only they could gain such victories and suffer such defeats!" (*SW*, I, 717). This patriotic idea, the key to understanding the entire tale, was of great importance to Karamzin, who was preparing to devote the next years of his life to a laborious but estimable objective—the writing of the *History of the Russian State*.

V *Disputes over Karamzin's Creative Writing*

> True scholars scorn both praise and abuse from the ignorant.
>
> —N. M. Karamzin

When Karamzin left the journalistic and publishing fields and concentrated all his efforts on his historical work, unusually sharp debates broke out over his creative writing. More and more people became involved in literary debates; the battle kept widening in scope. As a result, at the beginning of the nineteenth century the position of every writer was in many ways determined by the stand he took on Karamzin.

More or less personal or private differences of opinion over Karamzin's works appeared as early as the 1790's, but the really heated debates started in 1803 with the appearance of a book by Alexander S. Shishkov, *Rassuzhdenie o starom i novom sloge rossiyskogo yazyka* (*A Deliberation on the Old and New Style of the Russian Language*), in which the author took a sharp stand against Karamzin. Quoting an extract from *The Pantheon of Russian Authors* which dealt with the four epochs in Russian literature and the "pleasing style" of "the present time," Shishkov declared: "I have long wondered whether the writer of these lines was speaking in all sincerity or whether he was teasing us as a joke! What? He calls the absurdity of the present style—pleasant! An absolute disgrace and only damaging—yet he calls it an education!"[19]

Quite obviously exaggerating and distorting Karamzin's views, Shishkov blamed him for desiring to throw overboard his own language and establish a new one on the rules of the French language. Shishkov was an enemy of all borrowings from other languages. He censured "present-day writers" who "mar the language by introducing foreign words such as, for example: *moral'nyi* ("moral"), *esteticheskii* ("esthetic"), *epokha* ("epoch"), *stsena* ("scene"), *garmoniia* ("harmony"), *aktsiia* ("action"), *entuziazm* ("enthusiasm"), *katastrofa* ("catastrophe"), and so on."[20] These words, which Karamzin introduced, had gained a foothold in the Russian literary language, and Shishkov's objections proved only that he lacked a feeling for the language. True, Shishkov's book had its merits, and some of its ideas later evoked a response from so-called "archaists," including such prominent and talented writers as Pavel A. Katenin, Wilhelm K. Küchelbecker, and Alexander S. Griboedov.[21] For example, Shishkov raised a very important point— the question of vernacular speech and its role in the literary language. Sentimentalists were distinguished by their great purism with respect to the lexical nature of popular speech, avoiding the use of words which, in their view, might spoil the "pleasing" style. Shishkov protested, championing the cause of authors who adopted a protective regard for the vernacular. Berating contemporary authors for their scorn of idiomatic language, Shishkov accused them of being guilty, not only of misusing the language, but of being unpatriotic as well.

However, with respect to Karamzin, such accusations were completely unjust. It is enough to recall his articles in *The Messenger of Europe* especially devoted to problems of national culture. The polemics between Karamzin and Shishkov arose over their opposing conception of the tasks facing writers.

While Karamzin and his followers worked out new principles of stylistics, creating a "middle style" more or less suitable for works of the most diverse genres, Shishkov tried to uphold Lomonosov's theory of "three styles" (high, middle, and low), preserving in the literary language even those Slavisms which were already considered out of date and archaic by the end of the eighteenth century.

On this point, there could not be any agreement at all with Shishkov. Indeed, Karamzin was quite candid in pointing out that when he had made up his mind "to appear on the scene, I could not find a single Russian author worthy of imitation and, while I give full credit to the eloquence of Lomonosov, I could not help noticing his wild and barbarous style, not at all appropriate to the present taste, so I tried to make my writing more lucid and more lively. I had in mind certain foreign authors; at first, I imitated them, but afterwards I wrote in a style of my own which I borrowed from nobody."[22]

Karamzin, however, did not make a personal reply to Shishkov's *Deliberation*, but those who shared his views did write to the press. P.I. Makarov, publisher of the journal *Moscow Mercury*, printed a rather lengthy article criticizing Shishkov's book. The author of the *Deliberation* printed his response to the criticism, which was followed by new polemical attacks by other writers, some defending Karamzin, others supporting Shishkov.

The polemics concerned literary style, but from the very beginning of the controversy it was clear that other problems stood in back of the question. "In rebelling against Karamzin and his followers," wrote N. I. Mordovchenko, who made a thorough study of the literary fracas at the time, "Shishkov had no scruples in expressing his doubts about their religious and patriotic feelings. Thus, the question of 'old' and 'new' style was shifted onto social and political grounds almost from the moment it was posed."[23]

Actually, even before Shishkov's book appeared, serious doubts regarding Karamzin had been voiced by Andrey Turgenev, the talented, well-educated son of the Mason Ivan P. Turgenev. In March 1801, in a speech before the Friendly Literary Society (Druzheskoe literaturnoe obshchestvo)—a group of writers and men of letters who tried to link their writing activities with the propagation of civic and patriotic ideas—young Turgenev bitterly remarked that one could learn very little about the Russian people from the works of Russian writers.[24] Passing on to a critique of Karamzin, Turgenev gave him credit where it was due, admitting that "Karamzin [had] created an epoch in our literature," but further on, the young author declared:

He has overpersuaded us to be mild and soft. He should have been born a century earlier at a time when there were more artistic works in the most important genres—then he could have woven his flowers into our native oaks and laurels. I'll put it plainly: he has done our literature more harm than good; yet, with the same sincerity, I'll admit that I myself—and probably I'm not alone in this—would rather have written what he has than anything belonging to all our epic poets. The fact that, in his way, he writes so beautifully makes him even more harmful; it would be better if Russians wrote worse, though in not so interesting a manner, if only they would take up topics that are most important; better if they would write with more originality and, what is more vital, not stick so much to secondary genres. . . .[25]

Andrey Turgenev belonged to a new generation, being fifteen years younger than Karamzin. His speech was full of polemic fervor and full of the desire to work out a new literary program quite independently. However, Andrey Turgenev's critique of Karamzin's writing was made from an entirely different point of view in comparison with that of Shishkov. Whereas the author of the *Deliberation* had expressed the protective ideas of pseudo-patriotism, demanding abstention from any kind of borrowings, Turgenev did not at all reproach Karamzin for his "Europeanism." It is significant that Turgenev, unlike Shishkov, highly appreciated Karamzin's artistic talent and even admitted that he himself would have liked to write like the famous author. But Turgenev was convinced that Karamzin's creative works did not meet the most essential needs of Russian literature, and he fought for reviving genres with heroic and patriotic themes and for creating works distinguished by greater national originality. These demands were well founded, and similar opinions were later expressed by writers from among the revolutionaries of the aristocracy who criticized Karamzin's fiction even more severely.

Despite his youth, Andrey Turgenev managed to make quite a profound and objective analysis of the contemporary literary scene. He hit the mark when he said that "Karamzin would have had a more beneficial influence if crowds of rash imitators had not followed him from the moment he appeared on the scene."[26]

And certainly, at the end of the 1790's and beginning of the 1800's, more and more epigones of Sentimentalism appeared who tried to imitate Karamzin. Scores of mediocre writers, as well as those without any talent at all, produced works that were closely modeled after Karamzin's tales, verses, and his *Letters of a Russian Traveller*. They not only took their plots and individual motifs from Karamzin's works, but tried to copy his particular style and repeated his

116   NIKOLAY KARAMZIN

favorite expressions. But lacking Karamzin's education, culture, and
talent, their painstaking imitations often resembled parodies.
   Naturally, followers of this kind annoyed Karamzin no less than
his avowed enemies, and he has been quoted as having spoken
disdainfully of one of them, Vladimir V. Izmaylov: "In Izmaylov's
letters I noticed some commas he copied from me; but it is pardon-
able—he hasn't read anything in Russian, outside of *My Trifles*."[27]
   Many critics of the 1800's were well aware of the differences
between Karamzin and his imitators. A good example of this is
found in a review by the poet Ivan M. Born, author of the book
A Short Guide to Russian Literature (1808), who wrote the following
on Karamzin: ". . . The prose of this writer has, in effect, established
a new epoch in our literature; it apparently serves as a common
example for our young writers. But I must admit that, against his
will, this writer shares the same lot as the Englishman Sterne, whom
many also imitated and do even now, only with rather indifferent
success. I ask you, why should anyone with brains and a good
command of his native language, stick so slavishly to the style of
another writer?"[28]
   In addition to rejecting Karamzin's imitators, Born had two other
points: he did not consider Karamzin's creative work "harmful"
and he did not regard Karamzin's writings as belonging to a bygone
period, but kept in mind the fact that Karamzin's works were still
"in everyone's hands" and still being read avidly.
   The fight against the pseudo-Karamzins was prolonged by critics
who retained a deep respect and admiration for Karamzin himself,
drawing attention to the prodigious scope of Karamzin's literary
activity and creative search in comparison with that of his imitators,
who had stopped at a certain level, never going beyond the limits of
a definite thematic and stylistic sphere.
   Karamzin's literary style changed to coincide with the evolution of
his social, philosophic, and esthetic views. Victor D. Levin, a Soviet
linguist specializing in the stylistics prevalent at the end of the
eighteenth and the beginning of the nineteenth centuries, noticed
"a certain increase of 'Slavic' elements in Karamzin's works
written in the first decade of the nineteenth century."[29] Certainly, the
writer's style adopts new features in *A Historic Word of Praise to
Catherine II, Marfa-posadnitsa*, and a number of other works.
Most of the assertions made by critics who blamed Karamzin for
the "delicate" style in his earlier works could not be supported if

they were to refer to the works he published in *The Messenger of Europe*. Attempts by Shishkov and a few other literary opponents of Karamzin to accuse the writer of having no patriotic feelings were shown as being clearly groundless when the public was introduced to the *History of the Russian State*.

CHAPTER 6

History of the Russian State

I *The Work of a Historiographer*

> The Present is a consequence of the Past. To assess
> the former, one must remember the latter; the one,
> so to speak, rounds out the other, and by interlocking
> them the mind has a clearer picture of both.
>
> —N. M. Karamzin

DURING his European tour, Karamzin travelled to Paris in 1790
and had the opportunity to meet the French historian Pierre-
Charles Levesque, who had written a *History of Russia* (1782–83).
When describing this encounter later on in his *Letters of a Russian
Traveller*, Karamzin remarks with bitterness: "It hurts, but in all
fairness it must be admitted that up to now we do not have a good
history of Russia—that is, one written with a philosophic mind, critically, using the richest language." At this point he states his views as
to how a history of Russia should be written: "Tacitus, Hume,
Robertson, Gibbon—here are examples! They say that our
history, in itself, is less interesting than that of other countries.
I do not think so; only intellect, taste, and talent are needed. One
could select, enliven, add color, and the reader would be surprised
that something interesting and strong could be made of Nestor,
Nikon, and the like; something worthy of note not only for Russians,
but foreigners, too" (*SW*, I, 415).

The idea of writing a history of Russia, which had occurred to
Karamzin long ago, now gradually changed from the abstract
into a more concrete and practical form. The historical articles
in *The Messenger of Europe* show that Karamzin had already
accumulated materials and documents on Russian history. In
addition, his articles and, in particular, his tale *Marfa-posadnitsa*
showed his ability "to select, enliven, add color."

However, the writer could not publish the journal so demanding
of time and attention and simultaneously indulge his wish to start
work on the history. After consulting first with Dmitriev, Karamzin

decided in September 1802 to write to M. N. Muravyov, then Deputy Minister of Enlightenment [Education]: "I can and want to write a history that will not call for the work to be done in haste or within a fixed time," he wrote, "but I still do not have the means to live, without falling into great need."[1] Thanks to Muravyov, a man of brilliant education who was devoted to science, Karamzin's letter did not go unheeded and was followed by an order from the Emperor dated October 31, 1802, appointing Karamzin histori- ographer with a stipend of two thousand rubles a year. The writer could now retire from journalistic work and devote himself entirely to the monumental task which had lured him for so long.

The opening of this new stage in Karamzin's creative career coincided with another important event in his life—his second marriage. On January 8, 1804, he married Ekaterina Vyazemskaya, a clever and charming woman. In winter they lived in Moscow; in summer they went to the Vyazemsky's estate, Ostafievo, where, in a modestly furnished study, Karamzin spent most of his time working on the *History*. The more he delved into it, the more clearly he realized how difficult and time-consuming it was.

As a historian, Karamzin was not without predecessors. He could refer to works on Russian history written in the eighteenth century by Mikhail V. Lomonosov, Vasily N. Tatishchev, I. N. Boltin, Nikolay I. Novikov, and Prince Mikhail N. Shcherbatov. In addition to using their works he turned to the original sources— the chronicles and other old documents. Karamzin was given per- mission to work in the archives of the Foreign Board and in monas- tery libraries. New and valuable finds were the result of his research. For example, in 1808, Karamzin wrote to N. N. Novosiltsev, Muravyov's successor, that he had found thirteenth- and fourteenth- century manuscripts, hitherto unknown: "I can boldly and positively assert that I can [now] explain many things in our history that were obscure, although worth inquiry—and without resort to conjec- ture or invention."[2]

As he worked on the first volumes of the *History*, Karamzin already envisioned in rough outline the subsequent course it would take. The original synopsis—an essay on Russian history in concise form—is preserved in his paper entitled: *Zapiska o drevney i novoy Rossii* (*A Memoir on Ancient and Modern Russia*). The incen- tive to write it came in 1809 when the writer was introduced to the Grand Duchess Ekaterina Pavlovna, sister of Alexander I.

Karamzin visited her in Tver and read her some chapters from the *History*. Ekaterina Pavlovna was greatly interested in the work of the historiographer and had many talks with him about history and contemporary politics. She suggested that he write down his ideas so that Alexander could become acquainted with them. Karamzin obliged by writing *A Memoir on Ancient and Modern Russia* in 1811.

The epigraph to the work was chosen from the psalms: "There is no flattery on my tongue"—words reflecting the sincere and bold character of the *Memoir* meant for the Emperor. Karamzin briefly recounts Russian history from its early beginnings to the latest period.[3] For him, the transition from past to present was perfectly integrated, since historical events did not interest him as such, except to provide examples indispensable to present times. Karamzin tried to trace a certain natural process in Russia's historical development and considered that unification of the Russian state around Moscow was Russia's "glorious resurrection." Further, he spoke of consolidation under a one-man rule—autocracy—which, from his point of view, was salutary for Russia. A review of the past brought him to the conclusion that "Russia was founded on victories and on one-man leadership; she was perishing from divided rule, but saved by wise autocracy."[4]

However, while claiming that monarchical rule was beneficial, Karamzin set high standards for the sovereign. He made a sober and critical summary of the activities of the tsars, including those who reigned in the eighteenth century—the immediate predecessors and close relatives of Alexander I—Catherine II and Paul I. As he approached his own times, his skepticism grew. Trying to be as impartial as possible, he nevertheless gave Alexander I his due for remaining "a man on the throne"—a human sovereign—once the writer's monarchical ideal. But this still proved insufficient for the happiness and prosperity of the Russian people, and on becoming convinced this was true, Karamzin decided to speak openly to the Emperor. He declared that "Russia is full of the discontented; people complain both in palaces and huts; they have no confidence in nor zeal for the authorities and severely denounce their aims and measures."[5]

He dwelt at length on various aspects of economic and political life in contemporary Russia, proving that the new laws introduced by Alexander I and the newly established institutions were unsound.

Drawing a vivid picture of the bad organization prevailing throughout the country, Karamzin depicted the flourishing of bribery, bureaucracy, serious faults in educational matters, and the granting of titles and awards to unimportant and unworthy persons. "This criticism," writes one literary critic, "was not directed against the acts of the government of Alexander I by the Right, by a reactionary. The *Memoir* merely underscored the true picture of the disastrous situation in Russia where complete control was given over to governors—to fools and robbers, to corrupt police officials and judges."[6]

Karamzin's *Memoir* was documentary in scope and, at the same time, a brilliant, publicistic work illustrative of his artistic talent. Whether he was expounding on Russia's history or speaking of contemporary times, he repeatedly expressed his personal views on related events and facts. Despite its brevity, the reader could easily grasp Karamzin's sympathies. Partially using the traditions of Russian homiletic literature and guided by his previous experience as a publicist, Karamzin constructed his *Memoir* in the form of a dramatic monologue which rang with great emotional force.

Of course, there could be no thought of publishing such a work. Despite Karamzin's appeal to the magnanimity of Alexander I, the Tsar, after having studied the *Memoir*, reacted with clear displeasure. Later, relations gradually improved between the historiographer and the royal family, but Karamzin always managed to preserve his independence and self-respect. Thus, upon receiving the Emperor's offer to settle in the Anichkov Palace in St. Petersburg, Karamzin declined, writing his brother, V. M. Karamzin, on April 12, 1811: "It is a great favor; however, my dear brother, I am not at all thinking of moving to St. Petersburg. My connection with the imperial family must be one of disinterest. I want neither titles nor money from the Emperor."[7]

The war of 1812 forced him to abandon his work on the *History*. After sending his wife and children to Yaroslavl, he remained in Moscow and left the city only on the eve of its occupation by Napoleon's troops. The entire library that Karamzin had collected over many years perished in the Moscow fire, and the loss complicated his work as historiographer. Returning to Moscow in 1813, he resumed work once more, continuing earnestly to collect and incorporate new material. When the first eight volumes were ready, Karamzin decided publication should begin, which meant moving to St. Petersburg, where he spent the last years of his life. The appearance of the first volumes of *Istoria gosudarstva rossiyskogo (History of the Russian State)* in 1818 was a great event in Russian cultural life. Varied reactions to it by Karamzin's contemporaries were inevitable,[8] but certainly no readers remained indifferent. They argued over the *History* and eagerly anticipated its continuation.

The volumes that followed were greeted with growing enthusiasm, although the polemics intensified between those for and those against Karamzin. Meanwhile, he tenaciously worked on proof-reading and correcting the volumes to be published. He became seriously ill while at work on the twelfth volume and died on May 22 (June 3—New Style), 1826, without completing it.

His history came to an end before he had reached the eighteenth century, but his pen brought Russia's distant past to life.

New editions of the *History of the Russian State* enjoyed continuous success throughout the nineteenth century, and even today it attracts numerous readers at home and abroad.

II   *The People and the Sovereign*

> There is no government which is not in need of the people's love to be successful.
>
> —N. M. Karamzin

The questions which stirred Karamzin throughout his entire creative career did not cease to interest him when he began work on the *History*, and in the *History* Karamzin found new answers to questions that had engrossed him earlier. His interest in the morals, history, and culture of different nationalities, so evident in his work as publisher of the *Moscow Journal*, assumed a decided direction by the time he had begun work on *The Messenger of Europe*. Karamzin was primarily attracted to his country's past; therefore, his attention was concentrated on studying the peculiarities of the Russian national character. He had witnessed the events of 1812 in which the Russians displayed exceptional heroism in their fight against Napoleon's army. The general surge of patriotism also embraced Karamzin, who regarded his work on the *History* as an act of patriotic duty and devotion to his fatherland. He stressed this in his introduction to the first edition: " ... A

Russian name has a special charm for us: my heart beats quicker over a Pozharsky [a hero in Russia's fight against the Polish invaders in the sixteenth century] than over a Themistocles or a Scipio."[9]

Karamzin believed that his *History* would be conducive to strengthening the feeling of national consciousness, and with this in mind, his narrative was focused on questions of national interest. Just as his *Memoir on Ancient and Modern Russia* included a lesson to the reigning monarch using the past as an example, so the *History of the Russian State* invariably compared the present, directly or indirectly, with the past. Using historical sources, Karamzin continued to study political, social, and moral problems which were directly related to the times when the *History* was written.

A republic or an autocracy? An old question for Karamzin, and finally he clarified it in the *History*. Relating the early beginnings of the Russian state, he wrote: "Weak, divided into small regions before 862 A.D. according to the Nestorian calendar, our fatherland owes its grandeur to the happy introduction of monarchical power"(*HRS*, I, 115).

In depicting further historical developments, Karamzin resolved to show that monarchical rule had proven beneficial in preserving and consolidating a state power capable of safeguarding Russia's independence. The idea of a united state, essential in understanding *Marfa-posadnitsa*, was worked out far more consistently in the *History*.

However, not all his contemporaries were ready to accept the historiographer's monarchical views. Karamzin's *History* particularly aroused indignation and protest among certain liberals from the nobility, who—years later—participated in the uprising against tsarism in December 1825. The *History* met with objections, jeers, and even accusations of being "despicable"[10]—not only the first eight volumes appearing in 1818, dedicated to Alexander I, but the work as a whole. Karamzin was also accused of writing a history of the state instead of a history of the Russian people.

Certainly the main landmarks in Karamzin's history were the reigns of the various monarchs. But this did not mean that the historiographer was concerned only with sovereigns and their retinues. Each monarch's activities interested Karamzin only insofar as they affected the fate of the whole of Russia, the fate of the Russian people. While he remained an adherent of enlightened autocracy—typical of thinkers of the eighteenth century—Karamzin nevertheless attached great importance to the people's views. For instance, in speaking of the reign of Elena, the wife of Tsar Vasily Ioannovich (Vasily III) and mother of Ioann Vasilyvich (Ivan IV), Karamzin observed that Elena's unworthy conduct aroused the hate and contempt of her subjects. The people's silent condemnation of Elena was fraught with serious danger, as the historiographer shows: "The people were silent in the 'stognakh' [the squares], only to speak all the more—where tyrants cannot reach, in the close circles of family and friends—about the calamity of seeing lust on the throne" (*HRS*, VIII, 45).

In his depiction of Godunov's rule, Karamzin points out that Boris, a clever and adroit politician, spared no effort to gain public support. He noticed with alarm the sad faces in the crowds, was worried about the "common talk," and was ready to go to any length "to win the hearts and the imagination of the people" (*HRS*, X, 128).

Resolved to become Tsar, Boris went out of his way "to seem less of a usurper in the eyes of the people" (*HRS*, X, 228). Godunov was perfectly aware that the success of a ruler ultimately depends on how the people regard him. The people stand out as a powerful force: the sovereign must take them into account, for they determine his very destiny, and Karamzin dwells at length on those events in which the Russian people displayed heroism, courage, and patriotism.[11]

The people are referred to in the *History of the Russian State* in a collective sense. Sometimes Karamzin speaks of certain definite social strata: "boyars," "merchants," "the church," "officials and citizens," but more often he simply says "the people" or "rossiyane" (the Russians). When he speaks of Russia's relations with other countries, he often uses the plural "we," having in mind the nation as a whole.

One often finds the names of people who are neither members of the nobility nor connected with royalty, yet are glorified for their feats of daring or exceptional nobility of character. For example, there was Ermak, conqueror of Siberia, who possessed "wisdom, great valor, and decisiveness"; and Vasily Shibanov, a follower of Prince Kurbsky, who fearlessly delivered his master's letter to Ivan the Terrible and "with magnanimous stoicism" endured all kinds of torment.

The writer considered one of the "people's virtues" to be humility—a capacity for obedience. Depicting Ivan the Terrible's tyrannical rule, Karamzin gives several examples of the amazing meekness of the Tsar's subjects silently enduring the most vicious tortures. For amusement, Ivan the Terrible impulsively cut off an ear of one of his army commanders, who did not express indignation or offer resistance, but thanked the Tsar for his charity. Karamzin's comment is: "Such was the Tsar; such were his subjects! Should we be most surprised at him or at them? If he excelled in torturing, then they excelled in their patience" (*HRS*, IX, 262).

Incidentally, these words were written by the very same person who a few years before had declared in his poem *Tacitus* (1797), referring to the decline of Rome:

> In this very Rome, once famous for heroism,
> Nothing but murderers and victims do I see.
>   Yet pity would be quite misplaced:
> It earned the cruel strokes of its sad destiny
> Enduring what could not be borne were it not so debased.

(CPW, p. 239)

Wondering about a possible limit to endurance and patience—a point beyond which "baseness" begins—was one of the questions occupying Karamzin during the years he worked on his *History*. He had to face facts which caused him to frame conflicting attitudes. For example, after the murder of Tsarevich Dimitry, the lawful heir, by Boris Godunov's hirelings, a people's revolt broke out in Uglich, and the townspeople themselves dealt swiftly with the Tsarevich's murderers. To Karamzin, this revenge seemed just, as it was the people who punished the criminals. At the same time, in the view of the historian, the people acted unlawfully, breaking "civil laws," and, therefore, were guilty before the state court (*HRS*, X, 135). All must obey the law: both subjects and sovereign; and Karamzin was deeply convinced that any violation of the law was a crime against one's fatherland. If observance of established laws contributed to the country's welfare, then any digression from the law could be harmful and even ruinous. But, he pointed out, subjects could be made to obey the law; a sovereign could only be persuaded.

III   *Portraits of the Tsars*

An imaginary, transparent curtain of secrecy does not
conceal the weaknesses of the head that wears the
crown.

—N. M. Karamzin

The *History of the Russian State* ended not merely as a collection
of chronological historical information, but as a work of creative
thinking by a writer of great experience.

In illustrating the conduct of state figures, Karamzin always
tried to reveal inner stimuli, but to do so, it was imperative to understand the peculiar nature and psychology of each person under
discussion. Naturally, many things in history remain unknown or
unclear, but despite the wealth of his imagination, Karamzin did
not consider it possible to introduce invention or fantasy into the
History. The only way was to gather all the material available in
order to make the picture as complete as possible. In selecting,
arranging, and developing this information, Karamzin displayed
the taste and talent of a creative writer who could depict, by means
of a few individual touches, living and memorable portraits of
diverse historical personages.

Of the innumerable characters appearing in the *History of the
Russian State*, attention is drawn especially to Ioann IV (Ivan the
Terrible) and Boris Godunov. The volumes depicting their reigns
were exceptionally successful and were read with greater eagerness
than works of fiction. Dramatic situations, intrigue, passion, and the
portrayal of the people's sufferings and misfortunes were all vividly
described in Karamzin's work.

Carefully selecting commentaries by Ivan's contemporaries,
records of annalists, and other available material, Karamzin succeeded in showing the complexity and contradictions inherent in
the personality of Ivan the Terrible as he followed the evolution of
Ivan's character over many decades.

Orphaned early, Ivan had no wise tutors; the boyars surrounding
him were concerned only with winning the trust and favor of the
Tsarevich, amusing him, and carrying out his every wish. One
document of an eyewitness, quoted by Karamzin, tells how Ivan, "in

love with the hunt . . . enjoyed not only the killing of wild animals but the tormenting of domestic pets, hurling them to the ground from high galleries. And the boyars would say: 'Let his Majesty enjoy himself!'" (*HRS*, VIII, 77).

The ruinous result of such an upbringing soon made itself felt even in the first years of the reign of Ivan, who "loved to show himself a tsar, not in matters of wise management but through executions [and] unbridled caprice" (*HRS*, VIII, 93). Yet Karamzin does not pass silently over those deeds of Ivan that deserved approval or praise. Thus, he speaks of Ivan's magnanimity at the beginning of his reign, about the Tsar's ability to rise above personal offense and not pursue revenge, and about his bravery during the great fire in Moscow.

In contrast to the chroniclers who were witnesses to the drastic change that took place in Ivan—the "strange storm"—Karamzin explains it as having been "not a sudden thing, of course, this burst of rage in a soul once so devout; the progress of good or evil happens gradually" (*HRS*, IX, 20).

He was convinced that the chroniclers had not noticed what was seething in Ivan's soul—"the struggles between his conscience and mutinous passions." Karamzin's brief remarks about the odious change in Ivan permitted the reader to interpret the facts from a completely different point of view; and further events depicted by the historian take on a new shade of meaning which is non-existent in the annals.

At one time a great admirer of the Swiss philosopher Lavater, Karamzin later became rather skeptical of phrenology or, more exactly, physiognomy; yet he still took an interest in studying how a person's external appearance reflected his inner life. Describing Tsar Ivan's appearance in detail, he draws attention to the change in his "once pleasant face"—a transformation that occurred simultaneously with the "terrible change" in his soul: " . . . He was so changed that it was impossible to recognize him: on his face lay an expression of gloomy rage; all his features were distorted, his gaze dull; and hardly one hair remained on his head, or of his beard, from the inexplicable effect of the fury which seethed in his soul" (*HRS*, IX, 79).

Karamzin shows how Ivan lost his former nobleness and became a tormentor. The wickedness and injustice perpetrated by Ivan deprave him and lead to the moral degradation of his personality.

He becomes cowardly and pitiful, betraying a weakness of spirit in everything—the "debasement of tyranny," Karamzin profoundly and pointedly remarks. The complicated psychological problems set forth in the *History* are worked out later by the Russian Realists, particularly Fyodor Dostoevsky.

Karamzin's search for high moral standards and his reflections on inescapable retribution for unqualified wickedness and villainy are also evident in the *History* with the depiction of yet another tragic episode from Russia's past. This episode concerns the crime of Boris Godunov, who gave the order to kill the seven-year-old Tsarevich Dimitry, lawful heir to the throne. There is some doubt, though, as to the reliability of this fact. Karamzin himself in 1802 published an article in *The Messenger of Europe* entitled "Historical Recollections and Commentaries on the Path to the Throne," giving a fairly detailed account of Boris' rule. According to Karamzin, "If Godunov had not cleared the way to the throne by murder, then history would have called him a weak monarch; . . . his royal services were so great that the Russian patriot would like to entertain doubts of his evildoing. It is painful to loathe the memory of a man who had such an exceptional mind, who fought bravely against state disasters, and who passionately wished to earn the people's love!"[12]

Karamzin concedes that the story of the murder might be an invention and, standing by Godunov's tomb, he remarks: "What if we are casting slander on these ashes, what if we are unjust in pulling the memory of this man to pieces, believing false opinions put into the chronicles thoughtlessly or from hostility?"[13]

It is true that Karamzin did not deny the evidence of the chroniclers and recognized that "Godunov, blinded by passion, might have shed innocent blood and gained the throne by this terrible means."[14] But simultaneously the writer hastens to refute other accusations against Boris by historians who "were not ashamed to describe [him] as a mad villain."

However, in the years between the 1802 article and the volumes of the *History of the Russian State* which cover Boris' reign, a basic change took place in Karamzin's treatment of the Godunov story. The historiographer made a minute study of numerous historical documents and statements giving evidence; then, accepting the murder version, he depicted the event somewhat differently:

Under the shy and hesitant Tsar Fyodor Ivanovich, Boris Godunov—brother of Fyodor's wife, the Tsarina Irina—became the actual ruler of Russia. Godunov was clever and energetic; as Karamzin declared, he was "a citizen worthy of power" (*HRS*, X, 12). However, all the good and noble acts of Godunov lose their value, as they are only a means of achieving glory and power. Boris was unable to resist the temptation when the chance came of getting rid of the only lawful heir to the throne, though it meant committing murder. Unlike Ivan the Terrible, who took delight in the very act of evil, Godunov committed a crime because there was no other way to take power. But the murder of little Dimitry left a dark stain on all the acts of Godunov. The historian never failed to see selfish thoughts, hypocrisy, and clever political scheming behind everything Boris did, even though it seemed for the good of Russia.

True to his writing craft, evident in his early tales, Karamzin took his character's point of view in an effort to understand the inner motivation behind his every action. Depicting Boris' intention of killing the Tsarevich, the historiographer passes on Godunov's train of reasoning—his thoughts about how Fyodor's possible death would make Dimitry resent him. The reason was that the Tsarevich was under the influence of his mother and relatives who were barred from contact with the throne and consequently hated Godunov. Karamzin writes: "What awaits Irina, in such a case? The convent. And Godunov? A dungeon or the block—for him, whose nod could move the kingdom; for him, beloved by tsars of the East and the West! . . ." (*HRS*, X, 126).

The historian seems to speak through the mouth of Boris himself, who reveals his most secret thoughts and makes a confession. Godunov gets his wish and, on becoming Tsar, does all he can to win the love and gratitude of the people through good and useful pursuits. But the evil he committed weighs on him. He loses the gift of enjoying happiness because "truly glorified, truly loved, he no longer knew peace in his soul; now he felt that if greatness could be attained by lawlessness, then greatness and happiness, of the most earthly kind, were not synonymous" (*HRS*, XI, 96).

Alexander Pushkin underlined the bond existing between his tragedy *Boris Godunov* and Karamzin's *History*, with the following eloquent dedication: "This work is dedicated with veneration and gratitude to Nikolay Mikhaylovich Karamzin whose memory is precious to all Russians, and whose genius inspired me."[15]

Yet, Pushkin did not agree with the historian on everything;[16] besides, Pushkin had a totally different artistic aim in writing his tragedy, and therefore, his image of Boris Godunov was basically different from that of Karamzin, who had constructed his own Godunov from chronicles and contemporary reports. Karamzin's Godunov is restless and suffers from pangs of conscience, but he is not Pushkin's Godunov who seeks expiation for his sin.

IV   The Author's Image in Depth

> God sees whether I love humanity and the Russian people.
>
> —N. M. Karamzin

The author's voice echoes continually throughout the *History*: one time it bears an epic calmness, another time it rings with excitement, yet another time it is ironical. His more or less detailed moral and philosophic reflections occupy a place of importance, or, as Boris M. Eikhenbaum expressed it: "Long esthetic experience and philosophical thought went into Karamzin's *History*."[17]

Naturally, then, the image of the historian has much in common with the Karamzinian image which the reader acquires from reading *The Letters of a Russian Traveller*, and the tales and publicistic articles published in both the *Moscow Journal* and *The Messenger of Europe*.

The heroic patriotism typical of *Poor Liza, Natalya, the Boyar's Daughter* and the article *O Lyubvi k otechestvu i narodnoy gordosti* (*On Love for the Fatherland and National Pride*) was given a new accent and greater depth in the *History*. The historiographer referred to the "kindly legends of old" tenderly and lovingly; everything connected with his country's past was close to his heart; he was proud of the "great days of [Russian] military glory." Karamzin even speaks boldly of facts which could not have made him happy as a patriot. For example, telling of the evil doings of Ivan the Terrible "with reluctance," he does not omit even the most horrifying historical details of the tyrant's reign, as if certain that the truth would prove useful and necessary to the well-being of his fatherland.

Writing about the reign of Oleg (*ca.* 882–912 A.D.), the historian tells how Oleg, using deception, killed the Kievan princes, Askold and Dir, and immediately comments: "The barbarianism most common to those times does not excuse cruel and bloody murder" (*HRS*, I, 124). Concluding his narrative on Oleg's rule, he summarizes by giving Oleg his proper due as a military commander and ruler, then adds: "But the blood of Askold and Dir leaves a blemish on his fame" (*HRS*, I, 144).

The principle of evaluating a sovereign on the basis of his deeds and conduct gradually took on a more complex form as Karamzin continued working on the *History*. As before, the basic criterion was the well-being of the fatherland. Although he supported all matters that he felt were for the good of Russia, the historiographer began to discriminate between the practical results of a ruler's activities and his underlying aim, that is, the inner motives stimulating a given behavior. Concluding the history of Boris Godunov's reign, Karamzin recalls the "true verdicts for posterity of Boris' acts—his generosity, love for public education, zeal for Russia's greatness, his sane and peaceful policy." Despite all this, in the historian's view, "the name of Godunov, one of the wisest sovereigns in the world, has been spoken with loathing for centuries, and will be in the future, to the glory of strict moral justice" (*HRS*, XI, 181–82). Thus, all of Boris' farsighted achievements which benefitted Russia lost their value in Karamzin's eyes because he did not see them as Godunov's virtues. He was certain that "Boris would not, in any case, have had any hesitation in acting against his [own] wise state laws if his love for power had required him to make such a *volte-face*" (*HRS*, XI, 182).

The author of the *History of the Russian State* was a moralist who felt the influence of eighteenth-century philosophical ideas. The spiritual searches of the young Karamzin—resolved to find out how to reach true happiness, and dissatisfied with both the answers of the Masons and European thinkers—were continued throughout the author's writing career and reached a culminating point in the *History*. The idea of evaluating a person regardless of class and the idea that happiness does not consist of riches and honors were developed by Karamzin with surprising consistency. Whereas he was sometimes rather naïve in his Sentimental poems and tales, affirming the possibility of true happiness for the poor who lived in huts but followed the laws of virtue, in his *History* this question was reversed: power and wealth could not bring happiness to an unjust monarch. Here the Sentimentalist writer's moral criteria embraced a wider purport: from the limited sphere of private life, Karamzin passed over to social and political problems. But, as in his works of fiction, his attention in the *History* was primarily focused on man with his passions, virtues, and vices.

He informs about historical events, but also indicates how he feels about these events. The wise conduct of Boris is a "bright gleam for the mind," but it "chills" Karamzin's heart, for he knows Godunov's secret motives.

The author's comments are woven in and out of the narrative text. Indignant exclamations and rhetorical questions abound: Having related that Ivan had made the boyars guarantee that an escape would not be made, Karamzin observes: "A precaution useless and shameful on the part of a monarch, but this monarch was a tyrant!" (*HRS*, IX, 84). When he describes Boris' plan to kill the Tsarevich, he addresses a question to the reader: "Can there be such a thing as trust and sincerity in such a dastardly plot?" (*HRS*, X, 130).

The tone of emotional reportage prevailing in the author's style is sometimes replaced with biting irony. Karamzin does not pronounce open judgment on what arouses his indignation, but falls back on the craft he formerly employed in his tales. The hero of *My Confession* exposes his own worthlessness; his own words help the reader realize the moral poverty of his way of life. Karamzin makes use of the same stylistic gambit in the *History*, though here he seeks support from authentic documents, retaining the very words of real historical figures. For example, he included a letter from Ivan to Prince Kurbsky in which Ivan first speaks of his right to execute the guarantors without having to account for it.

He indiscriminately killed the old and the new nobility, "punishing the virtuous, punishing the wicked" (*HRS*, IX, 269). The villain, creating lawlessness at every step, nevertheless pretended that he was observing some sort of sham code of justice.

Throughout the narrative, the author of the *History* teaches the reader to distinguish the apparent from the real, to fathom the main point in political events, and not to be deceived by deceptive phrases. An experienced spinner of tales, Karamzin builds up a strong contact with the reader, ably preparing him to interpret correctly what he intends to speak of next. One of his favorite devices is to depict an event along two planes of view; first, how it looks externally, a long camera shot, regardless of its connection with other circumstances; second, a close-up to explore its inner meaning in comparison with other facts and the further course of history.

In essence, the author is the hero of the *History*, and the reader is always conscious of his presence in every volume. The author's image unites the chapters on different centuries and different personages and makes the multi-volume work a harmonious whole.

The language of the *History* played a significant role, arousing the critics' praise no less than did the contents of the work, and Karamzin himself considered this aspect of his work extremely important. Developing and perfecting the literary language was vital to him, and he believed that "by raising the spirits of the Russian people, victories, achievements, and state grandeur have a happy effect upon our very language which, used with talent and taste by intelligent writers, may today be the equal—in forcefulness, beauty, and charm—of the very best languages, ancient or modern" (*HRS*, I, 105).

Unquestionably, the imprint of its time marks Karamzin's *History of the Russian State*. Its author was limited in his world view by the conditions and circumstances of his epoch, and the modern reader can hardly share all aspects of his historical concepts and evaluations. Nevertheless, to his countrymen Karamzin continues to be an outstanding figure in the field of historical research, and his *History* will always remain a great monument in Russian literature, as well as in Russian historical writing.

CHAPTER 7

Conclusion

WHILE Karamzin was working on the *History*, his fictional works were republished in numerous editions and collections. Indeed, during the first two decades of the nineteenth century scarcely a literate person in Russia was unacquainted with Karamzin's works. But such wide recognition and popularity resulted in a threat to his position by the spawning of imitators who ultimately compromised the very concept of Sentimentalism.

Arguments were not always to the point in the sharp, mounting controversy between Karamzin's adherents and antagonists. His followers in many ways themselves distorted Karamzin's position, making it all the more vulnerable to attacks by anti-Karamzinists. The appearance of the *History of the Russian State* increased the bitterness of the controversy, but even those who valued the importance of the *History* thought that it was a thing apart from the rest of Karamzin's writings.

Biographical documents, letters, and comments by his contemporaries depict Karamzin as a man who tried to further the growth of national culture, who maintained his artistic independence, and who was not afraid to speak the truth to the Tsar. Writers of the following generation, the younger contemporaries of Karamzin, above all Alexander Pushkin, valued Karamzin as one "who greatly influenced Russian enlightenment and who contributed a number of important scholarly works." Vissarion G. Belinsky spoke highly of Karamzin, even at a time when his attitude to Karamzin's writings was highly critical.[1] Only later did it become evident that Karamzin's creative works were just as important to the development of Russian literature as his activities in enlightenment.

Increased interest in the genres of the historical tale and novel in nineteenth-century Russian literature was due largely to Karamzin's influence. His influence was similarly felt in other genres: tales about high society, travel diaries, and publicistic essays. A deep bond of continuity exists between Karamzin's creative works and those of the succeeding generations of Russian writers, primarily because of his elaboration of ethical and philosophical problems, and his introduction of psychological characteristics.

Recent studies devoted to Karamzin have emphasized his relationship to Pushkin and Tolstoy, and the list could include the names of Gogol, Dostoevsky, and many other Russian writers as well. Despite the differences between the artistic methods of the Sentimentalist Karamzin and the Realist writers, it can be seen how Karamzin's ideas, themes, plots, images, and craft devices were further developed in nineteenth-century Russian prose and poetry. It is enough to remember, for example, that the theme of the "little man"—so important to Pushkin, Gogol, and Dostoevsky—began with Karamzin's "Poor Liza."

In the twentieth century, Karamzin's influence has been limited mostly to a few Slavic writers—Bulgarian, Croatian, Ukrainian, and Carpathian. Karamzin's works have been extensively translated in Europe and America, and entire reviews and studies have been devoted to him.

Throughout all of Karamzin's works, the consistent development of certain philosophical, esthetic, and artistic principles can be traced. Karamzin's quest for a moral ideal began during his period of association with the Masons. His interest in the inner world of the individual and his resolve to understand the reasons for the triumph of good or evil in the human soul were all reflected in his poems, tales, and publicistic and historical works. The artistic images he created continue to attract readers, especially the unforgettable image of the author as the "sensitive" traveler, the lover of ancient Russia, and the ironical and clever spinner of tales.

Notes and References

Chapter One

1. P. N. Berkov, ed., *Problemy russkogo prosveshcheniia v literature 18-go veka* (Moscow-Leningrad, 1961), p. 9.

2. *Utrennii svet*, Part I (1777), p. viii.

3. L. B. Svetlov, *Izdatel'skaia deiatel'nost' N. I. Novikova* (Moscow, 1946), p. 61.

4. Peter Brang, "A. M. Kutuzov als Vermittler des westeuropäischen Sentimentalismus in Russland," *Zeitschrift für slavische Philologie*, No. 30 (1962), 44–57; Yurii M. Lotman, "*Sochuvstvennik* A. N. Radishcheva"; A. M. Kutuzov, letter to I. P. Turgenev in *Uchenye zapiski Tartuskogo universiteta*, vypusk 139, *Trudy po russkoi i slavianskoi filologii*, 6 (Tartu, 1963), 281–96.

5. V. Vernadskii, *Russkoe masonstvo v tsarstvovanie Ekateriny II* (Petrograd, 1917), p. 114.

6. G. N. Pospelov, "U istokov russkogo sentimentalizma," *Vestnik Moskovskogo universiteta*, No. 1 (1948), 6.

7. G. A. Gukovskii, "U istokov russkogo sentimentalizma," in *Ocherki po istorii russkoi literatury i obshchestvennoi mysli XVIII veka* (Leningrad, 1938), p. 251.

8. *Sobesednik lubitelei rossiiskogo slova*, Part 2 (1783), 129.

9. I. I. Dmitriev, "Vzgliad na moiu zhizn'," *Sochineniia Ivana Ivanovicha Dmitrieva* (St. Petersburg, 1893), p. 24.

10. Anthony G. Cross, "Various Idylls in Karamzin's Works," *Derzhavin i Karamzin v literaturnom dvizhenii XVIII–nachala XIX veka*, XVIII vek, Sbornik No. 8 (Leningrad, 1969), 210–28.

11. *Russkii arkhiv* (1863), p. 482.

12. P. R. Zaborov, "Ot klassitsyzma do romantizma," in *Shekspir i Russkaia kul'tura* (Moscow-Leningrad, 1965), pp. 72–75; A. G. Cross, "Karamzin and England," *The Slavonic and East European Review*, Vol. XVIII, No. 100 (December 1964), 93–94; Hans Rothe, *N. M. Karamzins europäische Reise: Der Beginn des russischen Romans*, Philologische Untersuchungen (Berlin-Zürich, 1968), pp. 55–65.

13. Nikolay M. Karamzin, *Izbrannye sochineniia v dvukh tomakh* (Moscow-Leningrad, 1964), II, 80. All subsequent references to this edition are indicated as *SW*, standing for *Selected Works*.

14. Gotthold Ephraim Lessing, *Emilia Galotti*, trans. by N. M. Karamzin (Moscow, 1788).

15. Regarding the importance of this journal, see: E. P. Privalova,

"Detskoe chtenie dlia serdtsa i razuma," in *Rol' i znachenie literatury XVIII veka v istorii russkoi kul'tury,* XVIII vek, Sbornik No. 7 (Moscow-Leningrad, 1966), pp. 254–60.

16. *Detskoe chtenie dlia serdtsa i razuma,* Part XVIII (1789), p. 165.
17. N. M. Karamzin, *Polnoe sobranie stikhotvorenii,* (Moscow, 1966), p. 59. All subsequent references to this edition are indicated as *CPW,* i.e., *Complete Poetical Works.*
18. "Songs of divine harpists ring with the power of inspiration."
19. R. D. Keil, "Ergänzungen zu russichen Dichter-Kommentaren (Lomonosov und Karamzin)," *Zeitschrift für slavische Philologie,* Vol. XXX, No. 2 (1962), 380–83; A. G. Cross, review of N. M. Karamzin, *Polnoe sobranie stikhotvorenii,* introduced and edited by Yurii M. Lotman (Moscow-Leningrad, 1966), in *The Slavonic and East European Review,* Vol. XLV, No. 105 (1967), 547.
20. Peter Brang, *Studien zu Theorie und Praxis der russischen Erzählung, 1770–1811,* Bibliotheca Slavica (Wiesbaden, 1960), p. 210.
21. *Detskoe chtenie dlia serdtsa i razuma,* Part XVIII (1789), p. 187.
22. *Ibid.,* p. 190.
23. *Ibid.,* p. 180.
24. K. A. Skipina, "O Chuvstvitel'noi povesti," *Russkaia proza: Sbornik statei* (Leningrad, 1926), pp. 13–41.

Chapter Two

1. *Moskovskie vedomosti,* No. 86, November 6, 1790.
2. Ia. L. Barskov, *Perepiska moskovskikh masonov XVIII-go veka* (Petrograd, 1915), p. 72.
3. "He is publishing for the public a journal which, without a doubt, is the worst that could ever be submitted to the educated world. He offers to teach us things which we never knew before." *Ibid.,* p. 86.
4. *Ibid.,* p. 29.
5. *Ibid.,* p. 99.
6. *Ibid.,* p. 2.
7. *Ibid.,* p. 197.
8. Gavriil R. Derzhavin, *Sochineniia s ob"iasnitel'nymi primechaniiami Ia. Grota,* 2nd ed. (St. Petersburg, 1868), Vol. I, 232.
9. *Moskovskii zhurnal,* Part 2 (1791), p. 281.
10. Karamzin, *Pis'ma N. M. Karamzina k I. I. Dmitrievu* (St. Petersburg, 1866), p. 22. Hereafter cited as *Letters to I. I. Dmitriev.*
11. Derzhavin, *Sochineniia,* I, 304.
12. On Dmitriev's poetry and his collaboration with the *Moscow Journal,* see: G. P. Makogonenko, "Riadovoi na Pinde voin," in *Poeziia Ivana Dmitrieva* (Leningrad, 1967), pp. 5–68.

13. In reality this is a work by Johann August Eberhard (1739–1809) given out as correspondence between the two philosophers. See: Hans Rothe, *N. M. Karamzins europäische Reise*, p. 125.

14. *Moskovskii zhurnal*, Part I (1791), 80.

15. *Ibid.*, Part VII (1792), p. 256.

16. *Ibid.*, Part II (1791), p. 205.

17. E. N. Kupreianova, "Russkii roman pervoi chetverti XIX veka," in *Istoriia russkogo romana v dvukh tomakh,* Vol. I (Moscow-Leningrad, 1962), p. 66.

18. *Moskovskii zhurnal*, Part I (1791), p. 357.

19. I. A. Kriazhimskaia, "Teatral'no-kriticheskie stat'i N. M. Karamzina v *Moskovskom zhurnale,*" XVIII vek, Sbornik No. 3 (Moscow, 1958), p. 274.

20. H. R. Brown, *The Sentimental Novel in America, 1789–1860* (New York, 1959), pp. 9–11.

21. *Sankt-Peterburgskie vedomosti,* No. 5, January 16, 1797, p. 86.

22. N. K. Piksanov, "*Bednaia Aniuta* Radishcheva i *Bednaia Liza* Karamzina," K bor'be realizma i sentimentalizma, in XVIII vek, Sbornik No. 3, (Moscow, 1958), pp. 309–25; J. L. Van Regemorter, "Deux images idéales de la paysannerie russe à la fin du XVIII siècle," *Cahiers du monde russe et soviétique,* Vol. IX (Janvier-Mars, 1968), 5–19.

23. Ivan A. Ivanov, *Sbornik statei, chitannykh v otdelenii russkogo iazyka i slovesnosti imperatorskoi Akademii nauk,* Vol. V, 2nd ed. (1873), pp. viii–ix.

24. On plot sources of the tale, see: L. V. Krestova, "Romanticheskaia povest'" N. M. Karamzina *Natal'ia, boiarskaia doch'* i russkie semeinye istorii semnadtsatogo veka," in *Drevnerusskaia literatura i ee sviazi s novym vremenem.* Issledovaniia i materialy po drevnerusskoi literature (Moscow, 1967), pp. 237–59.

25. Peter Brang, *Studien zu Theorie und Praxis . . .* , pp. 156–57; F. Z. Kanunova, *Iz istorii russkoi povesti (Istoriko-literaturnoe znachenie povestei N. M. Karamzina)* (Tomsk, 1967), pp. 93–94.

26. Peter Brang, "*Natalja, bojarskaja doč* und Tatjana Larina," *Zeitschrift für slavische Philologie,* Vol. XXVII, No. 2 (1959), 348–62.

27. S. P. Zhikharev, *Zapiski sovremennika* (Moscow-Leningrad, 1955), p. 438.

28. Karamzin, *Letters to I. I. Dmitriev,* pp. 5–6.

29. *Moskovskii zhurnal,* Part VI (1792), p. 6.

30. N. S. Tikhonravov, cited by L. V. Krestova in "Romanticheskaia povest'" N. M. Karamzina *Natal'ia, boiarskaia doch,*" *op. cit.,* p. 239.

31. *Russkii arkhiv* (1866), p. 1762.

32. V. I. Maslov, *Ossianizm Karamzina* (Priluki, 1928).

33. A. G. Cross, "Problems of Form and Literary Influence in the

Poetry of Karamzin," *Slavic Review,* Vol. XXVII, No. 1 (March 1968), 39–48.

34. Karamzin, *Letters to I. I. Dmitriev,* p. 10.

35. Richard Burgi, *A History of the Russian Hexameter* (Hamden, Conn., 1954), p. 74.

Chapter Three

1. V. V. Sipovskii, *N. M. Karamzin, avtor "Pisem russkogo puteshest-vennika"* (St. Petersburg, 1899); Hans Rothe, *op. cit.*

2. V. V. Sipovskii, *O literaturnoi istorii "Pisem russkogo puteshest-vennika"* (St. Petersburg, 1897), p. 92.

3. T. Roboli, "Literatura puteshestvii" in *Russkaia Proza,* ed. by Boris M. Eikhenbaum and Yurii N. Tynianov (Leningrad, 1926), p. 48.

4. G. P. Makogonenko, *Denis Fonvizin: Tvorcheskii put'* (Moscow-Leningrad, 1961), pp. 209–37.

5. Sergei N. Glinka, *Zapiski* (St. Petersburg, 1895), p. 88.

6. Ivan V. Lopukhin, *Izliianie serdtsa, chtishchego blagost' edinon-achaliia* (Moscow, 1794), p. 10.

7. Ivan I. Dmitriev, "Vzgliad na moiu zhizn'," in *Sochineniia,* Vol. XI (St. Petersburg, 1893), p. 59.

8. Nikolai I. Turgenev, "Rosiia i russkie," in *Vospominaniia izgnan-nika,* Vol. I (Moscow, 1915), p. 342.

9. Iurii M. Lotman, *Evoliutsiia mirovozzreniia Karamzina (1789–1803), Uchenye zapiski Tartuskogo Gosudarstvennogo universiteta,* Trudy istoriko-filologicheskogo fakulteta, Vypusk 51 (Tartu, 1957), p. 130.

10. N. I. Turgenev, "Rossiia i russkie," *op. cit.,* p. 342.

11. A. G. Cross, "Karamzin and England," *Slavonic and East European Review,* Vol. XLIII, No. 100 (December, 1964), 96–103.

12. E. N. Kupreianova, *"Russkii roman pervoi chetverti XIX veka," op. cit.,* p. 69–70.

13. Konrad Bittner, "Der junge N. M. Karamzin und Deutschland," in *Herder-Studien* (Würzburg, 1960), pp. 93–94.

14. See: K. F. Tiander, *"Labirint* Baggesen i *Pis'ma russkogo pute-shestvennika* Karamzina," *Datsko-russkie issledovaniia,* Vypusk 1, Zapiski istoriko-filologicheskogo fakulteta Sankt-Peterburgskogo universiteta, Part 108 (St. Petersburg, 1912), 1–138.

15. Christian Weisse (1726–1804), Johann Kramer (1723–88), and Johann Denis (1729–1800)—German poets, admirers of Gellert.

Chapter Four

1. A. Ia. Kucherov, ed., *N. M. Karamzin, I. I. Dmitriev, Izbrannye stikhotvoreniia* (Leningrad, 1953), p. 29; R. Lauer, "*Bezdelica*—ein literaturwissenschaftlicher Terminus?" in *Aus der Geistwelt der Slaven*. Dankesgabe an Erwin Koschmieder (Munich, 1967), pp. 167–68.

2. Mikhail P. Pogodin, *Nikolai Mikhailovich Karamzin po ego sochineniiam, pis'mam i otzyvam sovremennikov*, Materialy dlia biografii, Part 1 (Moscow, 1866), p. 216.

3. "Intelligent people, who cannot read my heart, will at least read my book," *Aglaia*, Part I (Moscow, 1794).

4. *Russkii arkhiv*, No. 11 (1890), p. 374.

5. Karamzin, *Letters to I. I. Dmitriev*, p. 61.

6. *Aonides*, Book 2 (Moscow, 1797), pp. ix–x.

7. *Ibid.*, p. x.

8. Karamzin, *Letters to I. I. Dmitriev*, p. 104.

9. For more details on Karamzin's attitude toward the French Revolution, see: Nikolai K. Gudzii, *Frantsuzskaia burzhuaznaia revoliutsiia i russkaia literatura* (Moscow, 1944), pp. 24–40; Iu. M. Lotman, "Otrazhenie etiki i taktiki revoliutsionnoi bor'by v russkoi literature kontsa XVIII veka," in *Uchenye zapiski Tartuskogo gosudarstvennogo universiteta*, Trudy po russkoi i slavianskoi filologii XVIII veka, VIII, Vypusk 167 (Tartu, 1965), 3–32.

10. G. P. Makogonenko, "Literaturnaia pozitsiia Karamzina v XIX veke," *Russkaia Literatura*, No. 1 (1962), 79. Philaletus in Greek—lover of truth; Melodorus—giver of songs, or, poet.

11. Alexander N. Radishchev, *Polnoe sobranie sochinenii*, Vol. I (Moscow-Leningrad, 1938), p. 127.

12. Alexander I. Herzen, *Sobranie sochinenii v 30-ti tomakh*, Vol. VI (Moscow, 1955), p. 12.

13. Iu. M. Lotman, "Russo i russkaia kul'tura vosemnadtsatogo veka," in *Epokha Prosveshcheniia, Iz istorii mezhdunarodnykh sviazei russkoi literatury* (Leningrad, 1967), p. 274.

14. L. I. Kulakova, *Ocherki istorii russkoi esteticheskoi mysli XVIII veka* (Leningrad, 1968), pp. 214–16.

15. N. M. Karamzin, *Razgovor o schastii* (Moscow, 1797), p. 5.

16. *Ibid.*, p. 19.

17. *Ibid.*, p. 76.

18. *Sbornik pesen i stikhotvorenii*, Manuscript Department of the Lenin State Library, Moscow.

19. For more about this variant of song, see: Natal'ia D. Kochetkova, "K istorii vospriiatiia poezii N. M. Karamzina," in *Studien zur Geschichte der russischen Literatur des 18. Jahrshunderts* (Berlin, 1970).

20. L. V. Krestova, "Drevne-russkaia povest' kak odin iz istochnikov povestei Karamzina," in *Issledovaniia i materialy po drevne-russkoi literature* (Moscow, 1961), p. 209.

21. Vadim E. Vatsuro, "*Ostrov Borngol'm* i 'goticheskaia' literatura," in *Derzhavin i Karamzin v literaturnom dvizhenii XVIII—nachala XIX veka*, XVIII vek, Sbornik No. 8 (Leningrad, 1969), pp. 190–209.

22. *Ibid.*, p. 206.

23. P. N. Berkov, "Zhizn' i tvorchestvo N. M. Karamzina," in *N. M. Karamzin—Izbrannye Sochineniia*, Vol. I (Moscow-Leningrad, 1964), pp. 38–39.

24. L. V. Krestova, "Povest' N. M. Karamzina *Sierra Morena*," in *Rol' i znachenie literatury vosemnadtsatogo veka v istorii russkoi kul'tury*, XVIII vek, Sbornik 7 (Moscow-Leningrad, 1966), pp. 261–66.

25. N. M. Karamzin, "Iuliia" (Moscow, 1796), p. 74.

26. Peter Brang, *Studien zu Theorie und Praxis . . .* pp. 171–75.

Chapter Five

1. N. M. Karamzin, *Istoricheskoe pokhval'noe slovo Ekaterine Vtoroi* (Moscow, 1802), p. 50.

2. *Vestnik Evropy* [*Messenger of Europe*, sometimes also translated as *European Herald*] Nos. 23–24 (1803), p. 283.

3. Vasilii V. Gippius, "*Vestnik Evropy*, 1802–30," in *Uchenye zapiski Leningradskogo gosudarstvennogo universiteta*, Vypusk 3 (Leningrad, 1939), 201–28.

4. V. G. Berezina, *Russkaia zhurnalistika pervoi treti XIX veka* (Leningrad, 1965), pp. 9–16; A. G. Cross, "N. M. Karamzin's *Messenger of Europe*—1802–3," *Forum for Modern Language Studies*, Vol. V, No.1 (January 1969), 1–25.

5. V. A. Teplova, "*Vestnik Evropy* Karamzina o velikoi frantsuzskoi revoliutsii i formakh pravleniia," in *Derzhavin i Karamzin v literaturnom dvizhenii XVIII—nachala XIX veka*, XVIII vek, Sbornik No. 8 (Leningrad, 1969), pp. 269–80.

6. G. P. Makogonenko, "Literaturnaia pozitsiia Karamzina v XIX veke," *loc. cit.*, pp. 87–89; Iu. M. Lotman, "Otrazhenie etiki . . . ," *op. cit.* pp. 27–31.

7. *Vestnik Evropy*, No. 20 (1803). pp. 319–20.

8. *Ibid.*, No. 22 (1802), pp. 144–45.

9. P. A. Orlov, "Respublikanskaia tema v zhurnale Karamzina *Vestnik Evropy*—K voprosu ob evoliutsii mirovozzreniia pisatelia," in *Philologicheskie nauki*, No. 3 (1969), 15–24).

10. *Vestnik Evropy*, No. 2 (January 1802), p. 75.

11. *Ibid.,* pp. 35–37.

12. *Ibid.,* No. 3 (February 1802), pp. 33–35.

13. Dieter Boden, *Das Amerikabild im russischen Schrifttum bis zum Ende des 19. Jahrhunderts* (Hamburg, 1968), pp. 51–52.

14. Iu. M. Lotman, "Puti razvitiia russkoi prozy 1800-kh–1810-kh godov," in *Uchenye zapiski Tartuskogo gosudarstvennogo universiteta, Trudy po russkoi i slavianskoi filologii,* No. IV (1961), 31.

15. F. Z. Kanunova, *op. cit.,* pp. 136–141.

16. V. I. Fedorov, "Istoricheskaia povest' N. M. Karamzina *Marfa-posadnitsa,"* in *Uchenye zapiski Moskovskogo gorodskogo pedagogicheskogo instituta imeni V. P. Potemkina,* Vol. LXVII, Vypusk 6 (1957), 109–29; P. A. Orlov, "Povest' N. M. Karamzina *Marfa-Posadnitsa,"* *Russkaia literatura,* No. 2 (1968), 192–201.

17. P. N. Berkov, "Zhizn' i tvorchestvo N. M. Karamzina," *op. cit.,* Vol. I, p. 51.

18. Iakov B. Kniazhnin, *Izbrannye sochineniia* (Leningrad, 1961), p. 303.

19. Alexander S. Shishkov, *Rassuzhdenie o starom i novom sloge rossiiskogo iazyka* (St. Petersburg, 1803), pp. 3–4.

20. *Ibid.,* pp. 23–24.

21. Iurii N. Tynianov, "Arkhaisty i Pushkin," in *Pushkin v Mirovoi literature: Sbornik statei* (Leningrad, 1926), pp. 23–121.

22. G. P. Kamenev, "Pis'ma S.A. Moskotil'nikovu," in E. A. Bobrov, *Literatura i prosveshchenie v Rossii v XIX v.,* Vol. III (Kazan', 1902), p. 143.

23. N. I. Mordovchenko, "Polemika o 'starom' i 'novom' sloge," *Russkaia kritika pervoi chetverti XIX veka* (Moscow-Leningrad, 1959), p. 78.

24. Iu. M. Lotman, "Stikhotvorenie Andreia Turgeneva 'K otechestvu' i ego rech' v 'Druzheskom literaturnom obshchestve,'" in *Literaturnoe nasledstvo,* Vol. LX, No. 1 (Moscow, 1956), 323–38.

25. *Russkii bibliofil,* No. 1 (1912), p. 29.

26. *Ibid.,* pp. 29–30.

27. G. P. Kamenev, *op. cit.,* p. 143.

28. I. M. Born, *Kratkoe rukovodstvo rossiiskoi slovestnosti* (St Petersberg, 1808), p. 161.

29. V. D. Levin, *Ocherk stilistiki russkogo literaturnogo iazyka kontsa XVIII—nachala XIX v.—Leksika* (Moscow, 1964), p. 295.

Chapter Six

1. M. P. Pogodin, *op. cit.,* Part II, p. 18.

2. *Ibid.,* p. 45.

3. Richard Pipes, *Karamzin's Memoir on Ancient and Modern Russia* (Cambridge, Mass.), 1959.

4. *Ibid.,* p. 9.

5. *Ibid.,* p. 44.

6. G. P. Makogonenko, "Literaturnaia pozitsiia . . . ," *loc. cit.,* p. 98.

7. M. P. Pogodin, *op. cit.,* Part II, p. 85.

8. V. E. Vatsuro, "Podvig chestnogo cheloveka, *Prometei,* Vol. V (Moscow, 1968), 8–51.

9. N. M. Karamzin, *Istoriia gosudarstva rossiiskogo,* Vol. I (St. Petersberg, 1816), p. xxiii. All subsequent references to this editition will be indicated as *HRS,* i.e., *History of the Russian State.*

10. S. S. Volk, *Istoricheskie vzgliady dekabristov* (Moscow-Leningrad, 1958); V. E. Vatsuro, "Podvig chestnogo cheloveka," *op. cit.,* pp. 17–28.

11. G. P. Makogonenko, "Literaturnaia pozitsiia . . . ," *loc. cit.,* p. 104.

12. *Vestnik Evropy* (August 1802), p. 303.

13. *Ibid.,* p. 304.

14. *Ibid.,* (September 1802), p. 38.

15. A. S. Pushkin, *Polnoe sobranie sochinenii* (17 vols.), Vol. VII (Leningrad, 1937), p. 3.

16. B. P. Gorodetskii, *Tragediia A. S. Pushkina "Boris Godunov," Kommentarii* (Leningrad, 1969), pp. 28–44; also, I. M. Toibin, "*Istoriia gosudarstva rossiiskogo* N. M. Karamzina v tvorcheskoi zhizni Pushkina," *Russkaia literatura,* No. 4 (1966), 37–48; also, I. Z. Serman, "Pushkin i russkaia istoricheskaia dramaturgiia 1830-kh gg" in *Pushkin, issledovaniia i materialy,* Vol. VI, Realizm Pushkina i literatura ego vremeni (Leningrad, 1969) , pp. 118–49.

17. Boris M. Eikhenbaum, *Skvoz' literaturu* (Leningrad, 1924), p. 38.

Chapter Seven

1. Vissarion G. Belinkii, *Polnoe sobranie sochinenii* (13 vols.), Vol. VII (Moscow, 1955), p. 135.

Selected Bibliography

PRIMARY SOURCES

1. In Russian:

A Memoir on Ancient and Modern Russia. The Russian Text. Richard Pipes, ed. Cambridge, Mass., 1959.

Istoriia gosudarstva rossiiskogo. 2nd ed. St. Petersburg, 1818–29.

Izbrannye sochineniia. Vols. I–VIII, Moscow, 1803–04; 2nd ed., Vols. I–IX, Moscow, 1814; 3rd ed., Vols. I–IX, Moscow, 1820.

Izbrannye sochineniia. Two vols. Moscow-Leningrad: Gosizdat khudozhestvennoi literatury, 1964.

Perepiska Karamzina s Lafaterom. Supplied by F. Waldman, arranged by Ia. Grot. St. Petersburg, 1894.

Pis'ma N. M. Karamzina k I.I. Dmitrievu. Ia. Grot and P. Pekarskii, eds. St. Petersburg, 1866.

Polnoe sobranie stikhotvorenii. Iurii M. Lotman, ed. Moscow-Leningrad: Sovetskii Pisatel', 1966.

Sochineniia Karamzina, 3 vols. St. Petersburg: A. Smirdin, 1848.

2. In English:

BOWRING, JOHN, ed. *Rossiiskaia Antologiia: Specimens of the Russian Poets with Preliminary Remarks and Biographical Notices.* 2nd ed. London, 1821.

———, ed. *Specimens of the Russian Poets.* London: Whittaker, 1823.

KARAMZIN, N. M. *Julia.* Tr. by Ann P. Hawkins. St. Petersburg, 1803.

———. *Russian Tales.* Tr. by J. B. Elrington. London, 1803.

———. *Selected Prose of N. M. Karamzin.* Tr. and with an intro. by Henry M. Nebel. Evanston: Northwestern University Press, 1969.

———. *Tales from the Russian.* Tr. by A. A. Feldborg. London, 1804.

———. *Travels from Moscow through Prussia, Germany, Switzerland, France and England,* 3 vols. Tr. by A. A. Feldborg. London: Badcock, 1803.

WIENER, L., ed., *Anthology of Russian Literature.* Vol. 2. New York, 1903.

SECONDARY SOURCES

1. In Russian:

BELINSKII, VISSARION G. *Polnoe sobranie sochinenii.* Vols. I, V, and VIII. Moscow: AN SSSR, 1953–59.

Selected Bibliography

145

BERKOV, P. N., ed. *Istoriia russkoi literatury XVIII veka.* Leningrad: Nauka, 1968.

―――.*Istoriia russkoi zhurnalistiki XVIII veka.* Moscow-Leningrad: AN SSSR, 1952.

BERKOV, P. N. and G. P. MAKOGONENKO. "Zhizn' i tvorchestvo N. M. Karamzina." In N. M. Karamzin, *Izbrannye sochineniia,* Vol. I. Moscow-Leningrad: Gosizdat khudozhestvennoi literatury, 1964.

DMITRIEV, IVAN I. "Vzgliad na moiu zhizn'." *Sochineniia.* 2 vols. St. Petersberg, 1893, pp. 1–152.

EIKHENBAUM, BORIS M. "Karamzin." *O Proze.* Leningrad: Khudozhestvennaia literatura, 1969, pp. 203–13.

GROT, IA. K. "Ocherk deiatel'nosti i lichnosti Karamzina." *Sochineniia,* Vol. III. St. Petersburg, 1901, pp. 120–66.

GUKOVSKII, G. A. "Karamzin." *Istoriia russkoi literatury,* Vol. V. Moscow-Leningrad: AN SSSR, 1941, pp. 55–105.

―――. "U istokov russkogo sentimentalizma." *Ocherki po istorii russkoi literatury i obshchestvennoi mysli XVIII veka.* Leningrad: Goslitizdat, 1938, pp. 251–98.

KANUNOVA, K. Z. *Iz istorii russkoi povesti—Istoriko-literaturnoe znachenie povestei N. M. Karamzina.* Tomsk, 1967, p. 188.

KOCHETKOVA, N. D. "Ideino-literaturnye pozitsii masonov 80–90kh godov XVIII v. i. N. M. Karamzin." *XVIII vek.* Sbornik, No. 6. Moscow-Leningrad: Nauka, 1964, pp. 176–96.

―――. "Poeziia russkogo sentimentalizma—N. M. Karamzin–I. I. Dmitriev." *Istoriia russkoi poezii v dvukh tomakh,* Vol. I. Leningrad: Nauka, 1968, pp. 163–87.

KUCHEROV, A. IA. "Esteticheskie vzgliady Karamzina." *Literaturnaia ucheba,* No. 3, 1936, pp. 72–86.

KULAKOVA, L. I. *Ocherki istorii russkoi esteticheskoi mysli XVIII veka.* Leningrad: Prosveshchenie, 1968, pp. 180–263.

KUPREIANOVA, E. N. "Russkii roman pervoi chetverti XIX veka." *Istoriia russkogo romana v dvukh tomakh,* Vol. I. Moscow-Leningrad: AN SSSR, 1962, pp. 66–85.

LOTMAN, IU. M. "Otrazhenie etiki i taktiki revoliutsionnoi bor'by v russkoi literature kontsa XVIII veka." *Uchenye zapiski Tartuskogo gosudarstvennogo universiteta,* VIII, Vypusk 167. Tartu, 1965, pp. 3–32.

―――. "Evoliutsiia mirovozzreniia Karamzina (1789–1803)." *Uchenye zapiski Tartuskogo gosudarstvennogo universiteta,* Vypusk 51. Tartu, 1957, pp. 122–62.

MAKOGONENKO, G. P. "Literaturnaia pozitsiia Karamzina v XIX veke." *Russkaia literatura,* No. 1, 1962, pp. 68–106.

MORDOVCHENKO, N. I. "Karamzin i ego rol' v razvitii russkoi kritiki." *Russkaia kritika pervoi chetverti XIX veka.* Moscow-Leningrad: AN SSSR, 1959, pp. 17–56.

MURATOVA, K. D., ed. *Istoriia russkoi literatury XVIII veka*. Moscow-Leningrad: AN SSSR, 1962.

ORLOV, P. A. "Literaturnaia programma 'Moskovskogo zhurnala' Karamzina." *Nauchnye doklady vysshei shkoly. Philologicheskie nauki*, I, No. 2, 1966, pp. 136–46.

———. "Respublikanskaia tema v zhurnale Karamzina *Vestnik Evropy*"— "K voprosu ob evoliutsii mirovozzreniia pisatelia." *Philologicheskie Nauki*, No. 3, 1969, pp. 15–25.

PETROV, A. A. *Pis'ma N. M. Karamzinu. Russkii arkhiv*, 1893, col. 473–86; 1866, col. 1756–63.

PONOMAREV, S. I. *Materialy dlia bibliografii literatury o N. M. Karamzine*. St. Petersburg, 1883.

POGODIN, M. N. *Nikolai Mikhailovich Karamzin po ego sochineniiam, pis'mam i otzyvam sovremennikov*, 2 vols. Moscow, 1866.

SIPOVSKII, V. V. *N. M. Karamzin, avtor "Pisem russkogo puteshestvennika."* St. Petersburg, 1899.

SKIPINA, K. A. "O chuvstvitel'noi povesti." *Russkaia proza*. Leningrad: Akademia, 1926, pp. 13–41.

TIKHONRAVOV, N. S. "Chetyre goda iz zhizni Karamzina." *Sochineniia*, 3 vols. Moscow, 1898, Part 1, pp. 258–75.

VATSURO, VADIM E. *Derzhavin i Karamzin v literaturnom dvizhenii XVIII–nachala XIX veka. XVIII vek*. Sbornik 8. Leningrad: Nauka, 1969.

———. "Podvig chestnogo cheloveka." *Prometei*, Vol. V. Moscow: Molodaia gvardiia, 1968, pp. 8–51.

VINOGRADOV, V. V. "Neizvestnye sochineniia N. M. Karamzina." *Problema avtorstva i teoriia stilei*. Moscow: Goslitizdat, 1961, pp. 221–368.

VISHNEVSKAIA, G. A. "Iz istorii russkogo romantizma (Literaturno-teoreticheskie suzhdeniia N. M. Karamzina na 1787–92gg.)" *Voprosy romantizma v russkoi literature. Uchenye zapiski Kazanskogo universiteta*, Vol. 124, No. 5., 1964, pp. 26–106.

2. In Other Languages:

BITTNER, KONRAD. "Der Junge Nikolaj Michajlovic Karamzin und Deutschland." *Herder-Studien*. Würzburg, 1960.

BRANG, PETER. *Studien zu Theorie und Praxis der russischen Erzählung, 1770–1811*. Bibliotheka Slavica. Wiesbaden: Harrassowitz, 1960.

CROSS, ANTHONY G. "Karamzin and England." *Slavonic and East European Review*, Vol. XLIII, No. 100 (December 1964), pp. 91–114. III, No. 4 (Winter 1969), pp. 716–27.

———. "Karamzin in English: A Review Article," *Canadian Slavic Studies* III. No. 4 (1969), pp. 716–27.

———. "N. M. Karamzin's 'Messenger of Europe' (*Vestnik Evropy*), 1802–3." *Forum for Modern Language Studies, 1969*. Vol. V, No. 1, (January 1969), pp. 1–25.

————. *N. M. Karamzin: A Study of his Literary Career, 1783–1803.* Carbondale: Southern Illinois University Press, 1971.

————. "Karamzin Studies: For the Bicentenary of the Birth of N. M. Karamzin (1766–1966)." *Slavonic and East European Review,* Vol. XLV, No. 104 (January 1967), pp. 1–11.

————. "Problems of Form and Literary Influence in the Poetry of Karamzin." *Slavic Review,* Vol. XXVII, No. 1 (March 1968), pp. 39–48.

DEWEY, HORACE W. "Sentimentalism in the Historical Writings of N. M. Karamzin." *American Contributions to the Fourth International Congress of Slavists.* The Hague, 1958, pp. 41–50.

GARRARD, JOHN G. "Karamzin in Recent Soviet Criticism." *Slavic and East European Journal,* Vol. XI, No. 4 (Winter 1967), pp. 464–72.

GRASSHOFF, HELMUT. "Zur Rolle des Sentimentalismus in der historischen Entwicklung der russischen und der west-europäischen Literatur." *Zeitschrift für Slawistik,* VIII, No. 4, 1963, pp. 558–70.

NEBEL, HENRY M., JR. *N. M. Karamzin: A Russian Sentimentalist.* The Hague-Paris: Mouton, 1967.

ROTHE, HANS. *N. M. Karamsins europäische Reise: Der Beginn des russischen Romans.* Philologische Untersuchungen. Berlin-Zürich: Verlag Gehlen, 1968.

Index